Contents

Preface — v

1 Extent and Importance of the Scriptures — 1

2 Suggestions on Reading and Studying the Scriptures — 6

3 The Latter-day Saint Edition of the Bible — 11

4 Principles and Methods of Marking the Scriptures — 15

5 Marking the King James Text — 26

6 Marking Chapter Headings — 30

7 Marking Footnote Entries Containing Capitalized Headings — 33

8 Marking Footnote Entries Containing Cross-References — 37

9 Marking Footnote Entries Containing Editorial Notes — 39

10 Marking Topical Guide Entries — 41

11 Marking Bible Dictionary Entries — 46

12 Marking the Joseph Smith Translation Section — 57

13 Marking the Gazetteer — 61

14 Marking the Maps — 65

15 Locating Books and Appendix Sections in the Bible — 72

Appendix A: Initial Listing of Topics Related to the Bible — 77

Appendix B: Locating the "GR," "HEB," "IE," "OR" Footnotes — 81

Appendix C: Location of "JST" Footnotes; Additional "JST" Excerpts — 88

MARKING THE SCRIPTURES

Suggestions for Understanding and
Using the New LDS Edition of the Bible

DANIEL H. LUDLOW

Deseret Book Company,
Salt Lake City, Utah
1980

Preface

An official of Cambridge University Press, publishers of approximately seventy percent of all the Bibles for Protestants in the world, stated that the publication in 1979 of the new Latter-day Saint edition of the King James Version of the Bible was the most significant event in Bible publication in over a hundred years.

I agree wholeheartedly with this evaluation and feel certain many millions of persons, now and in the future, will acclaim this edition of the Bible as the most important since the King James Version was initially published in 1611.

One of the purposes of this brief publication is to help the reader become acquainted with the contents of this new edition of the Bible.

It is also hoped this publication will—

1. Encourage and motivate more Latter-day Saints to read, study, and ponder the scriptures.

2. Help each reader of the scriptures to develop a meaningful personal system of marking and studying the scriptures.

3. Give the reader a better understanding of and appreciation for the new edition of the Bible.

4. Help missionaries, teachers, and others who use the scriptures extensively to gain greater insights into the value, extent, and importance of the scriptures.

5. Promote better scriptural scholarship among members of the Church.

Special thanks and appreciation are expressed to several people:

To Sharon Kirwan, a careful and competent typist and a good friend of several years.

To Merle Romer, for her friendly help in efficiently typing and retyping—and retyping—major segments of the manuscript.

To Gary Gillespie, a friend and colleague of several years and fellow traveler to Israel for six months, for thoughtfully reading and evaluating the manuscript.

To Eleanor Knowles, who served as editor representing Deseret Book Company, and who was closely associated with the preparation and publication of the Bible.

To Luene, an ideal companion and helpmate, for her deep love and understanding of the scriptures, for her helpful suggestions, and for the many hours she spent in checking and verifying countless references and footnotes.

To Michelle, who at fourteen is the only one of our nine children still living at home full time, for her understanding and help.

And finally and most importantly, to our Heavenly Father, whose words comprise the holy scriptures and who has promised to continue to give his children line upon line, precept upon precept, and example upon example, as they receive and live the truths he has already revealed.

1

Extent and Importance of the Scriptures

Literally millions of books exist in the world today, and new books are being published so rapidly that a person could not possibly read them all. Of these innumerable books, four should be of special interest to all Latter-day Saints: Bible (Old Testament and New Testament), Book of Mormon, Doctrine and Covenants, and Pearl of Great Price.

The scriptures are among the most important books and writings on the earth today. Tens of thousands who have read them are firmly convinced and testify that they contain the mind and will of our Heavenly Father as he has revealed his truths to his prophets.

Essentially the scriptures contain teachings from our Heavenly Father as revealed to his prophets by the power of the Holy Ghost. They also contain historical information concerning the reactions of earlier peoples to the teachings of the prophets and the relationship of God to those people.

Not all the truths of our Heavenly Father have been revealed to his prophets, and not everything revealed to the prophets is contained in the scriptures. Thus we should prize highly the relatively few scriptures we have, knowing that as we read and live them he will give us more; as he has promised: "For behold, thus saith the Lord God: I will give unto the children of men line upon line, precept upon precept, here a little and there a little; and blessed are those who hearken unto my precepts, and lend an ear unto my counsel, for they shall learn wisdom; for unto him that receiveth I will give more." (2 Ne. 28:30.)

The reception, publication, and distribution of these materials also await the faithfulness and diligence of the Saints in reading the present scriptures and living their truths.

After the Lord has revealed his truths to his prophets, he holds the prophets responsible for teaching the people and/or recording these revelations for the benefit of future generations. He then holds us responsible for reading and living what is taught and written by the prophets.

The scriptures are sometimes referred to as the "standard works" because they serve as a standard against which the doctrines and teachings may be tested.

All that we teach in this Church ought to be couched in the scriptures. . . . If we want to measure truth, we should measure it by the four standard works, regardless of who writes it. . . . This is the standard by which we measure truth. (Harold B. Lee, *Improvement Era,* January 1969, p. 13.)

It makes no difference what is written or what *anyone* has said, if what has been said is in *conflict* with what the Lord has revealed, we can set it aside. . . . We have accepted the four *standard works* as the measuring yardsticks, or balances, by which we measure *every man's doctrine.* (Joseph Fielding Smith, *Doctrines of Salvation,* Bookcraft, 1977, 3:203.)

By the *standard works* of the Church is meant the following four volumes of scripture: The Bible, Book of Mormon, Doctrine and Covenants, and Pearl of Great Price.

These four volumes of scripture are the standards, the measuring rods, the gauges by which all things are judged. Since they are the will, mind, word, and voice of the Lord (D&C 68:4), they are true; consequently, all doctrine, all philosophy, all history, and all matters of whatever nature with which they deal are truly and accurately presented. The truth of all things is measured by the scriptures. That which harmonizes with them should be accepted; that which is contrary to their teachings, however plausible it may seem for the moment, will not endure and should be rejected. (Bruce R. McConkie, *Mormon Doctrine,* Bookcraft, 1966, pp. 764-65.)

Someone has likened the scriptures to a treasure house with

numerous rooms, each room containing a treasure to bless our lives. However, we need keys of experience and understanding to help us unlock the secrets of these treasures and appreciate their value.

A remarkable thing about the treasure house of the scriptures is that each time we go back to them we can take additional treasures away with us to bless our lives and the lives of those with whom we associate. Thus, regardless of how many times we have read the scriptures, when we read them again we see principles and truths not seen nor understood before. The principles and truths we learn each time we read the scriptures will help us solve some problems we are facing at the time. Perhaps that is why we did not see nor understand the principles before—we did not have the problems then.

Brigham Young likened the scriptures to "a lighthouse in the ocean, or a finger-post which points out the road we should travel. Where do they point? To the fountain of light. . . . They are of God; they are valuable and necessary: by them we can establish the doctrine of Christ." (*Journal of Discourses* 8:129.)

All members of the Church know they should read the scriptures of the Church. The Lord has commanded it through both his ancient prophets and modern prophets.

President Spencer W. Kimball has stated: "No father, no son, no mother, no daughter should get so busy that he or she does not have time to study the scriptures." (*Ensign*, May 1976, p. 47.) He has also suggested an effective way of accomplishing the goal of reading all the volumes of scripture: "I ask all to begin now to study the scriptures in earnest, if you have not already done so. And perhaps the easiest and most effective way to do this is to participate in the study program of the Church. . . . Each of the standard works should be studied intensely in the year it is scheduled for study [in the adult curriculum of the Church]." (*Ensign*, September 1976, p. 5.)

Reasons why Latter-day Saints should read the scriptures, then, include the following:

1. The Lord commands it.
2. Present Church leaders encourage and urge it.
3. Principles in the scriptures help us solve some of our present problems.
4. Truths in the scriptures help us make decisions from an eternal perspective.

3

5. Stories in the scriptures help us understand other people and learn from their mistakes so we can improve our own lives.

6. Knowledge of the scriptures is critical to obtaining a testimony of our Heavenly Father and of his Son, Jesus Christ, who is our Savior and Redeemer.

7. Scriptures contain principles, teachings, and ordinances of the gospel that must be learned and obeyed if we are to regain the presence of God.

Why Are the Scriptures Not Read?

Why, then, do we not read, study, and ponder the scriptures as we ought to? Probably as many reasons exist for not reading the scriptures as there are people. And it is equally probable that few of the reasons are valid.

One possible reason is that we tend to rationalize when we hear our Church leaders urge the members to read and study the scriptures. We conclude that they are surely talking to others, not to ourselves. Concerning this point President Spencer W. Kimball has written: "Let me pause here to point out a common error in the mind of man—that is, the tendency, when someone speaks of faithfulness or success in one thing or another, to think 'me,' and when someone mentions failure or neglect, to think 'them.' But I ask us all to honestly evaluate our performance in scripture study." (*Ensign*, September 1976, p. 4.)

Another possible reason is that the adversary does not want us to read the scriptures. If we study the scriptures diligently we might learn that God is truly our Heavenly Father and that Jesus is the Christ, the divine Son of God. Also, we might learn from the scriptures principles of happiness and progression that, if applied in our lives, would help us achieve joy and eternal life. The devil does not want us to know and apply these truths, so he does everything he can to prevent us from starting to read the scriptures and to keep us from continuing to read the scriptures once we begin.

However, the major reasons we do not read, study, and ponder the scriptures are within ourselves, and until we resolutely decide to do something about it and then stick firmly to that resolution, we probably will not follow a regular program of daily scriptural study as President Kimball has urged. (See "How Rare a Possession—the Scriptures!," *Ensign*, September

1976, pp. 2-5.) The next chapter has hints and suggestions on how to commit yourself to an effective program of daily scriptural study.

2

Suggestions on Reading and Studying the Scriptures

Following are a few specific hints and suggestions on how one may read and study the scriptures.

1. *Desire and decide to read the scriptures.*

Until you definitely decide you are going to read the scriptures through completely, you will not do it. So many other things will seem to have a stronger claim on your time that you will find it easy to put off reading the scriptures. Decide firmly you are going to read *everything* in *all* the scriptures.

2. *Read daily, even if it is only a small amount.*

Commit yourself to a minimum daily schedule. Some recommend reading a certain amount of material each day, such as a chapter, a page, or five pages. Others recommend reading for a certain amount of time, such as ten minutes or a half hour. Suggestions are also made frequently concerning the best time to read—early morning, just before or after a meal, late evening. You know better than anyone else what the demands are on your time and the best time for you to set aside regularly; therefore, recognize that your schedule or the schedule of your family may well be different from the schedules of others. Be realistic when you set your schedule, then keep to it.

3. *Involve others in your decision.*

The larger the number of people who know of your decision to read the scriptures daily, the more difficult it will be to let them down by not reading the scriptures. Ask a few friends to inquire frequently how you are progressing with your resolution to read the scriptures daily. If you tend at first to procrastinate, you will soon discover it is easier and requires less time to read the scriptures than to explain to your friends why you are not reading them!

4. *Liken or apply the scriptures unto yourself.*

As you read, place yourself in the position of the person who originally received or wrote the materials, or put yourself in the position of one of the major personalities in the story. The Book of Mormon came alive for me as a boy when I became Sam and followed my more spiritual brother, Nephi, through the episodes recorded in First and Second Nephi. If you become involved with the story, the material will be more meaningful to you, and you will be able to remember it longer. In general, psychologists say we remember about ten percent of what we read, approximately thirty percent of what we see, and nearly eighty percent of what we do. Although these figures may vary considerably from topic to topic, it is a sound learning principle to *involve yourself* in the subject. As you read the scriptures, pause occasionally and ask yourself a question such as, How can I relate more fully to this particular incident or principle?

5. *Ponder the scriptures.*

Do not speed-read the scriptures the way you might a novel or other light reading. Pause frequently as you read the scriptures, and think deeply or reflect upon the principles being taught. Ask yourself such questions as, Why did the Lord want Isaiah to record this particular thing? What did John the Revelator see in his vision of the last days that would prompt him to use this analogy?

I find that when I get casual in my relationships to divinity and when it seems that no divine ear is listening and no divine voice is speaking, that I am far, far away. If I immerse myself in the scriptures the distance narrows, and the spirituality returns. (Spencer W. Kimball, address to seminary and institute personnel, Brigham Young University, July 11, 1966.)

6. *Learn the gospel from the scriptures.*

Our Heavenly Father has sent prophets into the world to teach us the gospel. Teachings of some of the earlier prophets comprise the scriptures or standard works; these should be searched to obtain the fundamentals of the gospel.

> I don't know much about the gospel other than what I've learned from the standard works. When I drink from a spring I like to get the water where it comes out of the ground, not down the stream after the cattle have waded in it. . . . I appreciate other people's interpretation, but when it comes to the gospel we ought to be acquainted with what the Lord says and we ought to read it. . . . (Marion G. Romney, address to seminary and institute coordinators, April 3, 1973.)

The Lord has indicated in this dispensation that what his living prophets speak "when moved upon by the Holy Ghost shall be scripture, shall be the will of the Lord, shall be the mind of the Lord, shall be the word of the Lord, shall be the voice of the Lord, and the power of God unto salvation." (D&C 68:4.) Thus the inspired teachings of the living prophets should be considered as scripture in learning the fulness of the gospel.

7. *Relate the principles in the scriptures to all other truths.*

The principles learned in the scriptures can be applied to many aspects of life. In actively searching for these relationships, not only do you learn more about the scriptures, but their truths also become more relevant to everything about you. Remember, the gospel of Jesus Christ embraces all truth wherever it may be found.

> The Bible, Book of Mormon, Doctrine and Covenants, and Pearl of Great Price, do not contain the wisdom of men alone, but of God. . . . What mattereth it though we understand Homer and Shakespeare and Milton, and I might enumerate all the great writers of the world; if we have failed to read the scriptures we have missed the better part of this world's literature. (George Albert Smith, *Conference Report*, October 1917, p. 43.)

8. *Study the scriptures systematically.*

The Savior has counseled us to "search the scriptures" diligently. (John 5:39.) At least once you will want to read each volume of scripture from beginning to end in order to become acquainted with its historical and cultural context. After that, develop a systematic program for studying the doctrines from the scriptures by focusing on one topic at a time. The Topical Guide section of the Bible will provide references of many related scriptures on particular topics; read these scriptures in context and learn their background so you can see more readily how the truths of that topic relate to other truths. If you have a major teaching position in the Church, the demands of the lessons might help you decide what subjects to study. Otherwise, you might want to review the alphabetical headings in the Topical Guide and study those topics of most interest or importance to you. By following these procedures, it is hoped that you will soon study all the essential doctrines of the gospel.

9. *Develop a meaningful marking system.*

As you read the scriptures, you will undoubtedly want to mark certain words, verses, or sections to emphasize them or to help find them again quickly. Make certain you mark (and/or color) in such a way that your purpose of marking will be realized; in other words, make certain your system of marking and coloring has special meaning *for you*. One of the purposes of this publication is to help you think through and implement an effective system of marking the scriptures.

10. *Live the principles of the scriptures.*

It is not enough to read the scriptures nor even to learn the great principles contained therein. You must learn to apply these principles in your daily life. As the scriptures and our living prophet have said, it is not enough to *say*—we must also *do*. Occasionally as you read the scriptures, you might pause and ask, How can I use these principles to become a better person and to solve some of the problems I am now facing?

One cannot receive eternal life without becoming a "doer of the word" (see James 1:22) and being valiant in obedience to the Lord's commandments. And one cannot become a "doer of the word" without first becoming a "hearer." And to become a "hearer" is not simply to stand idly by and wait for chance bits of information; it is to seek out and study and pray and comprehend. (Spencer W. Kimball, *Ensign*, September 1976, p. 2.)

Become acquainted with the language of the scriptures and the teachings of the scriptures. After you have done that, you have to live it. You can't learn the gospel without living it. (Marion G. Romney, address to seminary and institute coordinators, April 3, 1973, p. 5.)

11. *Teach the scriptures to others, including your family.*

We have been counseled by the Lord to teach one another the doctrines of the kingdom. (D&C 88:77.) The best way to learn something is to teach it to others. This truism is particularly helpful in learning the scriptures. Someone has suggested that the Church is the "teachingest" organization on the earth. The Church and its many priesthood and auxiliary organizations provide many opportunities for teaching (and thus learning) the scriptures. Also, we must not forget our major responsibility of teaching the gospel and the scriptures to members of our family.

I admonish you, O Israel, search the scriptures; read them in your homes; teach your families what the Lord has said; and let us spend less of our time reading the unimportant and often harmful literature of the day, and go to the fountain of truth and read the word of the Lord. (George Albert Smith, *Conference Report*, October 1917, pp. 41, 43-44.)

We must study the scriptures according to the Lord's commandment (see 3 Ne. 23:1-5); and we must let them govern our lives and the lives of our children. (Spencer W. Kimball, *Ensign*, September 1976, p. 5.)

12. *Reread the scriptures frequently.*

Too many people have never read the scriptures even once; others have read them, but feel their obligation to the Lord has then been fulfilled. The scriptures have been written for many purposes, one of which is to help us learn principles so we can solve our problems. Since we are continually having different problems to solve, we will never outgrow our need for reading and rereading, studying and restudying the scriptures.

I am convinced that each of us, at some time in our lives, must discover the scriptures for ourselves—and not just discover them once, but rediscover them again and again. (Spencer W. Kimball, *Ensign*, September 1976, p. 4.)

3

The Latter-day Saint Edition of the Bible

This publication is not the place to give a detailed history of the new Latter-day Saint edition of the Bible. The *Ensign* of October 1979 contains a brief account (pp. 9-18), and it is hoped that additional background information will be given in other articles and in future histories of the Church. Perhaps it is sufficient to say here that the First Presidency and the Council of the Twelve directed the project from the very beginning, including the development of all the instructional aids, and approved each section before final printing.

The publication of the Latter-day Saint edition of the King James Version of the Bible has been heralded both within and without the Church as one of the most important publishing achievements of this or any other century.

The major features of the new edition are listed briefly here; most of them will be discussed later in greater detail. A real appreciation and understanding of the significance of this new edition, however, will come only as you read, study, compare, and ponder the contents of this remarkable volume.

1. *King James Text.* The text for this edition of the Bible is the King James Version word for word, comma for comma, period for period. Thus, any marking systems you have developed for other KJV texts might be used here also. See chapter 5 for suggestions for marking the King James text.

2. *Chapter Headings.* Each chapter of the Bible in this new edition contains a descriptive heading that highlights the essential contents of that particular chapter. You will find it interesting and informative to read at least once all the chapter headings consecutively from beginning to end. This will provide you with a relatively quick overview of the contents of the various books of the Bible, indicating the extent to which Latter-day Saint doctrine is contained within the Bible, and demonstrating the depth and scope of the chapter headings. See chapter 6 for suggestions for marking the chapter headings.

3. *Footnote Entries.* The footnote entries in this new edition of the Bible might be divided into three major groupings:

a. Footnotes headed by or containing the following capitalized letters: GR, HEB, IE, JST, TG, OR. Such footnotes provide (1) helpful information from other translations of the Bible, including the Greek [GR], the Hebrew [HEB], and the Joseph Smith Translation [JST], (2) explanations of idioms and difficult constructions [IE], (3) references to materials in the Topical Guide [TG], and (4) clarifications of archaic English expressions [OR]. See chapter 7 for suggestions for marking the footnotes containing these capitalized headings.

b. Footnote entries containing cross-references to other scriptures. This edition of the Bible contains, for the first time, cross-references to the Book of Mormon, Doctrine and Covenants, and Pearl of Great Price. Footnotes in previous Bible editions have contained only scriptural cross-references to the Old Testament and New Testament, considerably limiting the value to Latter-day Saint readers. See chapter 8 for suggestions for marking footnotes containing scriptural references.

c. Footnote entries containing editorial notes. Teachings of modern prophets and research of current scholars help clarify some of the more difficult passages in the Bible. Such helpful explanations are included as special editorial notes in many of the footnotes. See chapter 9 for suggestions for marking such notes.

4. *Topical Guide.* The longest segment of the Appendix contains a "Topical Guide with Selected Concordance and Index" to the scriptures of The Church of Jesus Christ of Latter-day Saints. This 598-page section includes over 2,800 separate alphabetical entries of subjects of interest to Latter-day Saints.

Pertinent scriptures from all of the standard works are listed in the following order: Old Testament, New Testament, Book of Mormon, Doctrine and Covenants, and Pearl of Great Price. See chapter 10 for suggestions for marking these entries.

5. *Bible Dictionary.* The best of previous Bible dictionaries published by Cambridge University has been combined with inspiration and the best of LDS scholarship to produce the helpful and informative dictionary section of the Appendix (pages 599-793). The more than 600 entries in the dictionary include topics essential to an understanding of the Bible as well as subjects of special interest to Latter-day Saints. Suggestions for marking Bible Dictionary entries are found in chapter 11.

6. *Joseph Smith Translation.* Many excerpts from the Joseph Smith Translation (JST) of the Bible, frequently referred to as the inspired version, are included in this new edition. Brief quotations from the JST are included in the appropriate footnotes on pages where the quotations would normally appear, and excerpts too lengthy for inclusion in footnotes are found in a special section of the Appendix, pages 797-813. These excerpts are a valuable addition to the standard King James text and frequently provide inspired clarification and amplification of difficult biblical passages. For suggestions for marking the Joseph Smith Translation excerpts, see chapter 7 (footnote entries) and chapter 12 (entries too lengthy for inclusion in footnotes).

7. *The Gazetteer.* The Gazetteer (pages 817-26) contains alphabetical entries of place names and locations important to an understanding of both the Old Testament and the New Testament. Each entry contains references to specific maps and also indicates the grid position on those maps for ease in location. See chapter 13 for suggestions for marking Gazetteer entries.

8. *Maps.* A 24-page section of twenty-two excellent colored maps is found at the end of the Appendix. See chapter 14 for suggestions on marking the maps.

9. *Running Heads for the King James Text.* Another valuable feature of this edition of the Bible is the use of comprehensive running heads at the top of each page of biblical text. These running heads include the name of the book, the number of the chapter, and the first verse on the page, together with the number of any additional chapters on that page and the number of the last verse on that page. Thus, a quick glance at the top of the page provides you with the beginning point of the first verse

on the page (book, chapter, and verse) and the ending point of the last verse on the page (book, chapter, and verse). No suggestions are given in this publication for marking the running heads, as they are self-explanatory. The margin at the top of each page occasionally might be used for other notations.

4

Principles and Methods of Marking the Scriptures

The words *mark, annotate,* and *cross-reference* will be used several times in this publication, so perhaps it would be well to define them here.

Mark. As used in the sense of marking the scriptures, the word *mark* means "to designate, set apart, identify, distinguish" or "to indicate, express, or show by a mark or symbol." In a general sense, anything added to the printed scripture is considered a mark. Such marks might take the form of lines, circles, letters, numbers, symbols, or anything else tending to designate or distinguish. In this broad sense, annotating and cross-referencing are also forms of marking.

Annotate. Webster's unabridged dictionary lists the following definitions of *annotate:* (1) to make explanatory or critical notes on; to comment upon; (2) to make notes by way of explanation; to make remarks on a writing. Thus, *annotation* is "a remark, note, or commentary on some passage of a book, intended to illustrate or explain its meaning: generally used in the plural; as, annotations on the Scriptures."

The basic root word of *annotate* is *note*, which suggests the use of words. Therefore, in this publication the term "annotating the scriptures" refers to use of words in marking a particular scripture.

Cross-Reference. Any system that leads a person from one scriptural reference to another is referred to as cross-referencing. This might be accomplished by the use of a mark as simple as a straight line, or it might include the special use of words (annotating). Several methods of cross-referencing are employed in the Latter-day Saint edition of the Bible:

1. Superscripts (superscribed or raised letters) in the text correspond with numbers of footnotes that usually contain other references, definitions, or explanations.

2. Topical Guide (TG) entries list scriptures related to the subject of the heading.

3. Bible Dictionary entries frequently quote from or refer to scriptures related to the subject defined.

4. The "Harmony of the Gospels" entry in the Bible Dictionary (pages 684-696 of the Appendix) identifies corresponding scriptures from the four Gospels (Matthew, Mark, Luke, and John) pertaining to the major events and teachings of Jesus Christ.

One of the major values of the Bible is that it contains some of the most elaborate and thorough cross-referencing systems of any Bible. These should greatly aid users in relating and associating pertinent scriptures to each other.

How to Begin Marking the Scriptures

If you have not had previous experience in marking and annotating a Bible, it might be worthwhile to read the remainder of this publication before deciding finally how you will mark *your* copy of the scriptures. It is always easier to add to a marking system later than to erase something inserted too quickly without purpose or reason.

Principles basic to any marking system include (1) determining important items you want to find in the scriptures; (2) organizing (at least in your mind) the important teachings of the scriptures into significant and meaningful groupings; (3) developing a consistent marking system to be used throughout the scriptures so as to facilitate ready identification without undue distraction; and (4) selecting appropriate and distinctive colors if a coloring system is to be used.

1. *Determining important items to be marked.*

A possible place to begin developing an effective marking system for the text of the Bible would be to take several small index cards (about 3 x 5-inch) or blank sheets of paper. Write on each sheet a major principle, ordinance, teaching, doctrine, concept, idea, truth, etc., with notes regarding what is important about each. Your cards might contain such individual entries as the following:

Faith. What it is and how it works.

God. His nature, characteristics, and traits. How he relates to us and why he works this way.

Israel. History and origin of Israel. Story of the Twelve Tribes of Israel. The major kingdoms (and kings) of Israel.

Baptism. What is its purpose? Why is it necessary? How is it performed? Is authority necessary?

Divinity of Christ. Specific significance of *Firstborn* and *Only Begotten.* Meaning of *Christ* and *Messiah.*

Opposition. Forces of evil. Lucifer, the devil, Satan. The recurring conflict of good and evil.

2. *Organizing important teachings into significant groupings.*

After you have completed so many of these small cards that you become repetitious or start listing unimportant items, arrange the cards into common groups of related topics.

If you find that you have too few groups (perhaps five or fewer), you may be including widely differing topics within the same group. On the other hand, if you have too many (perhaps ten or more), you may find it difficult to tell exactly which group fits a particular idea. It is hoped that most of your ideas will be included in five to ten groupings.

You might then take larger sheets of paper and outline (with major headings, subheadings, etc.) the materials within the various groups. It might also be well at this point to read the chapter headings in the Bible. Undoubtedly the contents of the chapter headings will suggest other items to place in your outlines.

3. *Developing a consistent marking system.*

The actual marking of your scriptures should begin only after you have decided what areas you want to mark and have determined what marking system you plan to use. A fundamental principle to remember in developing a system for marking scriptures is to make certain it is *your* system. If the system you use does not make sense to you or have special meaning for you, it probably will not be effective.

Several possible systems of marking the scriptures will be suggested in this publication to help *you* decide which system *you* might use: underlining, vertical lining, bracketing, boxing or blocking, circling, shading, numbering. It is not anticipated you will use all the systems suggested (in fact, you may not use any of the suggestions); however, if such a listing helps you decide on a system best suited for you, one of the purposes of this publication will have been realized.

Another important principle to keep in mind as you develop *your* system to mark *your* scriptures is KEEP IT SIMPLE. Use only those marks which in your mind tend to designate, set apart, identify, or distinguish. Mark only those scriptures or items that you think are important. Using too many marks or too many different marking systems indicates you have not thought through carefully enough exactly what you want to accomplish in the marking of your scriptures. Marking too many scriptures or items on a page leads to confusion and keeps you from achieving one of the major purposes of effective marking: ready identification or setting apart.

Another principle of good marking is to use marking materials that are readily available and yet will permit quick identification and setting apart without drawing undue attention. Several types of materials might be used, including colored pencils, colored pens, colored cellophane paper, and colored adhesive tapes. However, colored pencils seem to be the most effective and yet least expensive method, so this will be the only method discussed.

4. *Selecting appropriate and distinctive colors.*

The use of different distinctive colors contributes significantly to an effective marking system. Following are a few ideas to consider in selecting colored pencils:

a. Colors should be distinctive and relatively bright. As many as eight different colors (and perhaps even as many as twelve) might be used; however, if more than eight are used, it is sometimes difficult to differentiate between the shades.

b. Pencil lead should not contain too much wax; any wax, in time, will bleed through the sheet, discolor the paper, and show through on the other side.

c. Pencil lead should be relatively soft. If lead is too hard, the point tends to rip the paper before a wide enough impression is made to be clearly seen. If lead is too soft, it blurs and spreads out too far. Easily erasable colored pencils often smudge and blur quite easily.

d. Pencil should be regular length (approximately 7½ inches or 19 cm) and standard diameter. Pencils shorter than normal are hard to keep track of and are quickly used up; longer pencils are awkward to use at first; thicker or thinner pencils do not fit standard pencil sharpeners and are also more difficult to use.

e. Quality and cost of the pencil should also be considered. Your purchase of the scriptures represents a considerable investment, and you are also going to invest a good deal of valuable time in marking and annotating the scriptures. Thus, it is hoped that the slight additional cost of quality colored pencils in marking your scriptures should not be a prohibitive factor.

You might want to try out different brands and qualities before deciding which ones to use, but when you decide, you should purchase at least two identical sets of pencils so you can be assured of having enough identical colors to complete your marking project.

Another important principle to consider is to use colors *meaningful to you* in identifying certain concepts or doctrines. Do not worry too much about what various colors might mean to others, but make certain the colors mean something distinctive to you.

I once purchased a set of eight colored pencils to mark a new copy of the Book of Mormon. I then asked myself, "What color should I use to mark or identify related concepts or doctrines?" I decided that the answer to my question centered on which of the eight colors would likely come to mind when I thought of those particular concepts or doctrines.

I listed the eight colors of pencils in the set. Then, thinking of the major teachings in the Book of Mormon, I wrote next to each color the ideas that immediately came to mind when I thought of that color. The results were as follows:

Purple: I thought of royalty. Since the priesthood is referred to as the "royal priesthood," I decided to underline in purple all references pertaining to such topics as priesthood and Church government; priesthood power, authority, keys, offices, and functions; Church offices and positions; destiny and purpose of the Church.

Blue: I had been in Israel many times, and the blue star of David on the flag of Israel came to mind. Thus, I decided to underline in blue all references pertaining to Israel, including its origin, history, scattering, and gathering; prophetic promises pertaining to Israel as a land, people, and chosen nation; Israel in the latter days.

Yellow: My first thoughts were of light and the sun. Jesus Christ is the Light of the world and the Son of God, and so I decided to mark in yellow all passages pertaining to Jesus Christ, such as both the conditional and unconditional aspects of the atonement, including his suffering for sin in the Garden of Gethsemane and his resurrection.

Orange: No concept came to mind for orange, but since orange is closely related to yellow, I decided to mark in orange those doctrines closely associated with Jesus Christ, such as the eternal plan of life and salvation, beginning with pre-earthly existence, purposes of mortality, life after death, possibility of godhood (including principles of exaltation).

Red: Since this color seemed to be closely associated both with yellow and orange, I decided to mark in red all references to basic principles, ordinances, and covenants of the gospel, such as faith, repentance, baptism, and receiving the gift of the Holy Ghost.

Green: I thought of spring or newness of life. God the Father is the source of all life, and so I decided to mark in green all scriptures pertaining to the nature, characteristics, and roles of the various members of the Godhead. This idea was expanded to include references to the nature, calling, and functions of translated beings and those who have already become gods.

Brown: I thought of the ground or the earth, something basic or fundamental, and so I decided to mark in brown the historical events important or basic to the story being told. Names, dates, places, and other historical pegs on which more important concepts might be hung were marked in brown.

Black: My first thoughts were of evil, wickedness, and the devil. Thus, I marked in black those references pertaining to the devil, Satan, the adversary, and to his nefarious purposes, designs, enticements, temptations, methods, powers, and imitations. Scriptural references to sons of perdition and other followers of Lucifer were also emphasized with black.

Again, I emphasize that it is important for *you* to decide what colors *you* are going to use in marking *your* scriptures. Simply because a particular color works well for one person in identifying certain concepts or ideas does not mean that color will be best for you in identifying those same concepts or ideas.

Methods of Marking the Scriptures

Possible methods of marking the scriptures are listed here to help you determine which method (or combination of methods) might best serve your purpose in marking particular scriptural references or other items, such as footnote and Topical Guide entries. Suggestions for possible use of colors with these marking methods will be discussed in later chapters.

Be selective in determining when you might best use each method or if you should use it at all.

Underlining

Characteristics:
1. Easy to use.
2. Widely used.
3. Can include quotations of any length from one word to whole chapters.
4. Combines well with vertical lining, bracketing, and/or boxing.
5. Does not interfere with printed material.

Caution: Do not overuse. Make certain lines do not show through on other side of sheet. Keep lines straight and neat.

13 <u>And God said unto Noah,</u> The end of all flesh is come before me; for the earth is filled with *^a*violence through them; and, behold, I will *^b*destroy them *^c*with the earth.

14 ¶ <u>Make thee an *^a*ark of gopher wood;</u> *^b*rooms shalt thou make in the ark, and shalt pitch it within and without with pitch.

Vertical Lining

Characteristics:
1. Does not interfere with printed material.
2. Draws attention quickly.
3. Usually not so serious if it shows through on other side.
4. Combines well with underlining, word circling, shading, and/or numbering.

Caution: This system of marking is so easy to use that it is often overused. It quickly loses its effectiveness unless combined with other methods.

Shading

Characteristics:
1. Quickly draws attention if used sparingly.
2. Combines fairly well with vertical lining, bracketing, or boxing.

Caution: Scriptures marked with this system often show through on other side of sheet. The system quickly loses effectiveness if used too frequently. It also uses up pencils more quickly!

14 The LORD *is* my *a*strength and song, and is become my *b*salvation.

15 The voice of rejoicing and salvation *is* in the *a*tabernacles of the righteous: the right hand of the LORD doeth valiantly.

16 The right *a*hand of the LORD is exalted: the right hand of the LORD doeth valiantly.

17 I shall not die, but live, and declare the works of the LORD.

18 The LORD hath chastened me sore: but he hath not given me over unto death.

19 Open to me the gates of righteousness: I will go into them, *and* I will praise the LORD:

*a*AND there shall come forth a *b*rod out of the *c*stem of *d*Jesse, and a *e*Branch shall grow out of his roots:

2 And the *a*spirit of the LORD shall rest upon him, the spirit of *b*wisdom and *c*understanding, the spirit of *d*counsel and might, the spirit of knowledge and of the fear of the LORD;

Bracketing

Characteristics:
1. Interferes only slightly with printed material.
2. Can be used either in the margins or in the text itself.
3. Can be used effectively for segments of one line to one page.
4. Combines well with underlining, word circling, shading, and/or numbering.

Caution: This system loses effectiveness when used with large segments of material unless combined with other systems.

29 So ye in like manner, when ye shall see these things come to pass, know that it is nigh, *even* at the doors.
30 Verily I say unto you, that this ᵃgeneration shall not pass, till all these things be done.
31 Heaven and earth shall pass a-way: but my ᵃwords shall not pass away.
32 ¶ But of that ᵃday and *that* hour knoweth no man, no, not the angels which are in heaven, neither the Son, but the Father.

Boxing or Blocking

Characteristics:
1. Neat in appearance.
2. Effective for segments of two or three verses, particularly on the same page.
3. Combines well with underlining, word circling, shading, and numbering.

Caution: This system loses effectiveness if used with large segments.

29 So ye in like manner, when ye shall see these things come to pass, know that it is nigh, *even* at the doors.
30 Verily I say unto you, that this ᵃgeneration shall not pass, till all these things be done.
31 Heaven and earth shall pass a-way: but my ᵃwords shall not pass away.
32 ¶ But of that ᵃday and *that* hour knoweth no man, no, not the angels which are in heaven, neither the Son, but the Father.
33 Take ye heed, ᵃwatch and ᵇpray: for ye know not when the time is.

23

Verse Circling

Characteristics:

1. Easy to use.
2. Neat in appearance.
3. Interferes only slightly with printed material.
4. Effective only for emphasizing segments of at least one verse.
5. Best used in combination with other systems, such as underlining, word circling, shading, and/or numbering.

Caution: This system of marking is so easy to use that it is often overused. It quickly loses effectiveness unless combined with other methods. If less than one verse is to be emphasized, this system must be used with another system.

Word Circling

Characteristics:

1. Easy to use.
2. Emphasizes effectively *if not overused.*
3. Probably should be used with some other method, such as vertical lining, bracketing, or boxing.

Caution: This system is limited in application. It emphasizes, but does not necessarily show relationships.

29 So ye in like manner, when ye shall see these things come to pass, know that it is nigh, *even* at the doors.

30 Verily I say unto you, that this *ᵃ*generation shall not pass, till all these things be done.

31 Heaven and earth shall pass away: but my *ᵃ*words shall not pass away.

32 ¶ But of that *ᵃ*day and *that* hour knoweth no man, no, not the angels which are in heaven, neither the Son, but the Father.

33 Take ye heed, *ᵃ*watch and *ᵇ*pray: for ye know not when the time is.

2 Behold, God is my salvation; I will trust, and not be afraid: for the LORD *ᵃ*JEHOVAH is my *ᵇ*strength and *my* song; he also is become my *ᶜ*salvation.

3 Therefore with *ᵃ*joy shall ye draw water out of the wells of salvation.

4 And in that day shall ye say, *ᵃ*Praise the LORD, *ᵇ*call upon his name, declare his doings among the people, make mention that his name is exalted.

5 *ᵃ*Sing unto the LORD; for he hath done excellent things: this *is* known in all the earth.

6 Cry out and shout, thou *ᵃ*inhabitant of Zion: for great *is* the Holy One of Israel in the *ᵇ*midst of thee.

Numbering

Characteristics:

1. Effective (a) if not too many numbers are used and (b) if the reader can quickly identify the significance of the numbers.
2. Most effective if related numbers appear on same page.
3. Best used in combination with annotating and other systems of marking.

Caution: This system probably has limited application. Same numbers on different pages might have different meanings, and numbers might be difficult to pick out if they are written in the text.

[a]AND there shall come forth a [b]rod ① out of the [c]stem ② of [d]Jesse, and a [e]Branch ③ shall grow out of his roots: ④

2 And the [a]spirit of the LORD shall rest upon him, the spirit of [b]wisdom and [c]understanding, the spirit of [d]counsel and might, the spirit of knowledge and of the fear of the LORD;

5

Marking the King James Text

The methods you select for marking and coloring the King James text probably will affect greatly your later decisions on what to do with the other sections of the new edition of the Bible. Thus, you may want to review and carefully consider the principles and methods of marking and coloring discussed in the preceding chapter before making any further decisions. You may even want to read the remainder of this publication before deciding how to mark and color the KJV text.

Principles of Marking the Text

Let's review some basic principles and thoughts to assist you in your consideration:

1. The text of the Latter-day Saint edition of the Bible is the exact text of the King James Version. Thus any marking and/or coloring systems you have used in marking other copies of the KJV can also be used in this edition.

2. It is better to develop a system gradually according to

need, rather than to begin with a system too elaborate and involved. Remember, it is easier to add marks and colors than to erase them.

3. The use of too many colors too extensively can defeat some of the major purposes of an effective marking and coloring system. Do not mark or color anything unless you have decided what that mark or color will mean to *you*.

The text of the Bible is so long (1,590 pages in the new edition) and contains so many concepts, principles, truths, and ideas, that one of your first tasks should be to organize and group these materials together as much as possible. You might want to follow the suggestion in chapter 4 of listing ideas from the Bible on small separate sheets and then organizing them into larger groups.

To help you start thinking about particular ideas and concepts related to the Bible, consider the following:

1. The Old Testament is essentially a history of an extended family (the house of Israel) during a period of relative apostasy. The first 2,000 years of history from Adam to Abraham are covered in only twelve chapters in the first book (Genesis). Before you have finished Genesis, you have read of the origin of Israel, have followed Joseph into Egypt, and are only one chapter away from meeting Moses. Subsequent Old Testament books (Exodus through Malachi) recount an overview of the history of Israel through the next 1,300 years (c. 1700-400 B.C.), through the period of the judges, the 120 years of the united kingdom under Saul, David, and Solomon, the divided kingdoms of Israel and of Judah, and the tragic stories of apostasy, scattering, and partial restoration, followed by further dispersion. Undoubtedly several of your interests in the Old Testament would center in or revolve around the house of Israel.

2. The New Testament is essentially the story of the birth, life, and mission of Jesus Christ and of the attempts of his apostles and others to bear witness of him and his gospel throughout that part of the world. Your interests in the New Testament undoubtedly would include the life and example of the Savior and the major contents of his teachings.

After making this suggestion in chapter 4, I decided to try it in relationship to the Bible (I had previously used it for the Book of Mormon). I wrote on small slips of paper different ideas concerning the Bible and its teachings as these ideas came to me—one idea per slip of paper. Then I put related topics together in common piles. In this instance, the ideas seemed to fall into ten different areas, although I plan to go through them again and again to get them down to seven or eight groupings.

27

Although I hesitate to share with you the ideas in my initial ten groupings for fear it might restrict and structure your thinking, I have decided to list them in Appendix A in case you might want to glance through them for ideas of your own. Don't even look at them, however, if you already have enough ideas of your own to begin your own lists.

If this book were a manual for a class and if I were the teacher and you the student, I would probably ask you to write down your ideas first, organize them into your groupings, and *then* look at the ideas and concepts grouped in Appendix A. The assignment would then be to organize all of these ideas (your own and the ones in Appendix A) into no more than eight groups. Now that you have *your* groupings, proceed to the next steps of selecting and developing an effective coloring and marking system for the KJV text.

Marking the Text

Eventually you will probably want to use several methods of marking the voluminous text of the King James Version. At first, however, you might want to restrict yourself to such simple techniques as underlining, vertical lining, and bracketing. These are effective and compatible with each other, but should be used sparingly. Later your underlining may extend into shading, and your bracketing into boxing, but at first reserve shading and boxing for really special scriptures and purposes.

Coloring the Text

After you have organized your ideas pertaining to the Bible into eight or so groupings, a possible next step would be to select a distinctive color for each of these groups. Be sure you have a definite reason in mind for selecting a particular color for a particular group; the one should remind you of the other. In other words, when you think of the group, you should immediately think of the color; and when you think of the color, you should immediately think of the group.

Annotating the Text

The notes used in annotating the scriptures can be placed in any margins on the page: left, right, upper, or lower. Usually the lefthand or righthand margins would be used if the note(s) can be written next to the pertinent word, sentence, or verse.

If a longer note is needed or if the note pertains to a general concept rather than to a specific word or verse, the upper or lower margins might be used. In such instances, it might be well to insert a distinguishing mark in the text itself or in the lefthand or righthand margins that would lead to the note at the top or bottom of the page.

Summary and Review

Personalize your groupings and your systems of marking, coloring, and annotating. The subjects you are most interested in and want to know more about from the Bible are probably not exactly the same as those of your friends or even of other members of your family. Inasmuch as it is *your* Bible you are marking, make certain the subjects you are emphasizing are organized into groupings that have special meaning and significance for you.

The marks also should have special meaning to you. Remember that it is better to undermark than overmark; you can always add additional marks as you read and re-read the scriptures, but it is very difficult to remove marks once they have been made. Your notes should be legible and should be located in the margins where they can be seen readily. And remember to use distinctive colors that are quickly identifiable.

6

Marking Chapter Headings

The system you select for marking and annotating the King James text can also be used for marking chapter headings. For example, if blue underlining is used to designate passages dealing with Israel (origin, scattering, gathering) in the King James text, then those sections of the chapter headings concerned with Israel would also be underlined in blue.

Following are other suggestions for marking chapter headings:

1. Underline the word *chapter* and accompanying number in a distinctive color; this will help you determine immediately where each new chapter begins.

2. Distinctively mark and/or color those sections of Old Testament chapter headings that refer to prophecies concerning (a) the first coming of the Messiah and (b) the second coming of the Messiah, including events of the last days and millennial conditions. As examples, review the headings of the following chapters:

a. *First Coming of the Messiah*

Genesis 3
Numbers 24
2 Samuel 7
Psalms 2, 8, 9, 16, 21, 22, 31, 40, 45, 67-69, 72, 89, 91, 110, 118, 132
Isaiah 6, 7, 9, 11, 22, 28, 40, 42, 49, 50, 53, 61
Jeremiah 33
Hosea 11, 13
Micah 5
Haggai 2
Zechariah 3, 6, 9, 11

b. *Second Coming of the Messiah,* including events of the last days and millennial conditions

Deuteronomy 4, 30, 33
Psalms 9, 48, 50, 97
Isaiah 1, 2, 4, 5, 10-14, 18, 24, 27, 29, 30, 32-35, 44, 51, 52, 54, 60, 62-66
Jeremiah 3, 16, 23, 25, 30-32, 50
Ezekiel 11, 16, 20, 34, 36-40, 47
Daniel 2, 7, 10-12
Hosea 1-3, 14
Joel 2, 3
Amos 8, 9
Obadiah 1
Micah 2-5, 7
Nahum 1, 2
Zephaniah 1, 3
Zechariah 2, 3, 8, 10, 12-14
Malachi 3, 4

3. Mark sections of New Testament chapter headings that refer to prophecies concerning the events of the last days, including the restoration of the gospel, the restitution of all things, and incidents pertaining to the second coming of Christ and millennial conditions. As examples, review the headings of the following chapters:

Matthew 24
Mark 13
Luke 17, 21
Acts 3
Romans 11
Ephesians 1, 2, 4
1 Thessalonians 4, 5

2 Thessalonians 1, 2
1 Timothy 4
2 Timothy 3, 4
2 Peter 3
Jude 1
Revelation 1, 4, 7-22

4. Mark those sections of chapter headings that are

concerned with basic teachings of the Church but are not commonly interpreted this way in standard biblical commentaries. As examples, note the following portions of selected chapter headings in Genesis:

Genesis 2: Prior spirit creation explained; Adam and Eve are married by the Lord

Genesis 3: The Serpent (Lucifer) deceives Eve; Her Seed (Christ) shall bruise the Serpent's head

Genesis 49: Judah shall bear rule until Shiloh (Christ) comes; His [Joseph's] branches (the Nephites and Lamanites) to run over the wall; The Shepherd and Stone of Israel (Christ) shall bless Joseph temporally and spiritually

The following chapter headings also include portions indicating a Latter-day Saint interpretation:

Old Testament	New Testament
Exodus 21	Matthew 18, 24
Deuteronomy 32, 33	Mark 3, 10, 12, 13
2 Samuel 7, 23	Luke 17, 21
1 Kings 7	John 1, 8, 21
2 Chronicles 4	Acts 3, 20, 27
Psalms 85, 108	Romans 5, 6, 9, 11
Proverbs 8	1 Corinthians 6, 8, 10-12, 15
Isaiah 2-14, 29, 33, 48, 49, 53, 54	Galatians 3
Jeremiah 23, 30, 33	Ephesians 1, 2, 4
Ezekiel 37	Colossians 1
Daniel 2, 7, 11	1 Thessalonians 5
Joel 3	2 Thessalonians 1, 2
Nahum 1	1 Timothy 4
Zephaniah 1, 2	2 Timothy 3
Zechariah 3, 6, 12-14	Hebrews 1, 3-5, 7
Malachi 3, 4	1 Peter 2-4
	2 Peter 3
	1 John 3
	Jude 1
	Revelation 2-4, 8, 12, 14, 15, 20-22

5. Mark the sections of Psalm 119 as though they were separate psalms. This psalm has a series of sections designated by the letters of the Hebrew alphabet, and headings have been prepared for each of them; thus the sections and their headings might be marked as though they were separate psalms.

7

Marking Footnote Entries Containing Capitalized Headings

A significant contribution in the footnote section is the inclusion of alternate translations of the Bible, explanations of idioms and difficult constructions, appropriate references to entries in the Topical Guide, and clarification of archaic English expressions. These are discussed on the page opposite the beginning of Genesis as follows:

Cross references to related passages throughout the standard works have self-identifying abbreviations for each book cited. Other abbreviations are as follows:

GR: An alternate translation from the Greek.

HEB: An alternate translation from the Hebrew.

IE: An explanation of idioms and difficult constructions.

JST: *Joseph Smith Translation.* Excerpts from the Prophet Joseph Smith's translation of the Bible. Short excerpts are provided in the footnotes; longer excerpts are provided in the Appendix. Italic type in these JST excerpts is used for words not found in the King James Version.

TG: *Topical Guide.* References to the 'Topical Guide with Selected Concordance and Index,' given by topic title. This material is in the Appendix.

The word 'OR' signifies that alternate words follow to clarify the meaning of archaic English expressions.

Each of the footnote entries relates to a superscript (a small superscribed or raised letter thus: ^{a}) in the King James text. The verse number and superscript appearing in a particular verse will begin the related footnote entry; you might want to mark and color (a) the superscript in the text, (b) the corresponding letter in the footnote, and (c) the capitalized letters in the footnote. In the following examples, possible colors are suggested to indicate what might be done; however, you should determine which color *you* feel will work best for *you.*

GR: An Alternate Translation from the Greek

The New Testament comes to us primarily from the Greek language. Thus, frequently the alternate translations from the Greek add significantly to a better understanding of the New Testament.

In determining what color to use in marking the footnote entries containing the abbreviation GR, let's try word association. What color, if any, comes to mind when you think of *Greek* and/or GR? Let's suppose your word associations are "Greek—GR—Green." You might then decide to mark all GR (Greek) footnote entries in green. To identify quickly the superscript in the text and the footnote, you might decide to mark them all in green.

A list of pages containing GR footnotes is found in Section 1 of Appendix B. This list should be of great assistance if you decide to mark the alternate translations from the Greek.

HEB: An Alternate Translation from the Hebrew

The Old Testament comes to us primarily from the Hebrew language or languages closely associated with Hebrew. Thus the numerous alternate translations from Hebrew add greatly to a better understanding of the Old Testament.

What color, if any, comes to mind when you think of the word *Hebrew*? Let's assume you previously decided to mark in blue references to Israel in the text; you might now decide to use blue to mark the Hebrew translations inasmuch as *Hebrew* and *Israel* are closely related. The superscript and corresponding letter and the HEB footnote entry then might be marked in blue.

A list of pages containing HEB footnote entries is found in

Section 2 of Appendix B. As you mark these entries, read the alternate translations from Hebrew in the appropriate place of the King James text and note the significant contributions.

IE: Idioms and Difficult Constructions

Every language contains idioms or idiomatic expressions that, by definition, indicate the meaning is peculiar to a particular group. Webster's unabridged dictionary defines an idiom as "having a meaning that cannot be derived as a whole from the conjoined meaning of its elements."

In American English, the following expressions (with their real meanings in parentheses) are idiomatic: "Tom had the heart of a lion." (This expression does not mean the heart of a lion has been transplanted into Tom. Rather, it means Tom is brave or courageous.) "Collins died on third base." (Very few baseball players actually suffer physical death while running the bases. The expression means Collins, the runner, did not score from third base before his teammates made three outs in that inning.)

An understanding of the real meaning of idioms in the Bible is critical to a better understanding of that holy scripture. Thus you will want to read in context, and probably will want to mark, all footnotes containing IE headings (in yellow, for "new light" or better understanding?). Remember to color the superscript number as well as the footnote. A list of pages containing IE footnotes is found in section 3 of Appendix B.

JST: Excerpts from the Joseph Smith Translation

Short excerpts from the Joseph Smith Translation of the Bible are provided in the footnotes; longer excerpts are provided in the Appendix of the Bible. Italic type in these excerpts is used for words not found in the King James Version.

You might want to mark these references in a distinctive bright color (red?) to draw attention to their importance. You might want to mark the italic words also. Remember to color the corresponding letter in the superscript and the footnote, and the capitalized letters JST. Verse numbers of JST and KJV are not always identical; thus, you might write in any verse numbers that are different so you can readily cross-reference the two texts.

Appendix C of this publication lists pages of the Bible containing JST footnotes and also has a selection of JST verses not cross-referenced in the new Bible edition.

Chapter 12 has suggestions on marking the longer JST excerpts found in the Appendix of the Bible (pages 797-813).

TG: Topical Guide

An important feature of the new edition of the Bible is the inclusion of the Topical Guide section of the Appendix. This section is discussed more fully in Chapter 10, with suggestions on how to mark entries within the Topical Guide.

Literally thousands of footnote entries on the 1,590 pages of biblical text refer to the Topical Guide. In fact, superscripts and footnotes leading to the Topical Guide are so numerous that you might want only to underline them rather than to use a more extensive marking system. You might also select a color that will not draw undue attention to itself (brown, for "tan ground"—TG?). Because the TG footnote entries are so numerous, a separate listing of them has not been prepared.

OR: Alternate Words to Clarify Archaic English Expressions

Many English words have changed meanings since the King James Version was first printed in 1611. Footnote entries with the capitalized word OR help to clarify in modern English what was meant by a particular English word when it was used originally.

You might want to use orange (for OR) for the superscripts and the footnotes.

A list of pages containing footnotes headed by OR is found in section 4 of Appendix B.

8

Marking Footnote Entries Containing Cross-References

Most of the footnote entries include cross-references to other scriptures. Any marking system involving the coloring of such scriptures should be limited; otherwise the footnote sections would have so many colored entries that some of the basic principles of effective marking (quick location and identification) would be lost. Some color marking might be used to accomplish special purposes, however. Following are two suggestions:

1. *Mark scriptural references essential to understanding.*

One possibility of marking the scriptural references in the footnote entries would be to underline only those scriptural references essential to full understanding of the passage.

As an example, in Genesis 50:25, Joseph had the children of Israel promise they would carry his bones out of Egypt when they returned to the promised land. The footnote entry pertaining to this verse (25b, page 78) refers to Exodus 13:19 (Moses takes Joseph's bones out of Egypt) and Joshua 24:32 (Joseph's bones buried in Shechem). These additional scriptural references are necessary to complete the meaning of Genesis 50:25 and to show that the desires of Joseph were carried out. They might be distinctively marked.

As another example, Numbers 21:9 indicates that Moses, in response to a command from the Lord, "made a serpent of brass and set it upon a pole" in order that his people might look upon it in faith and live. The footnote of the verse (9a, p. 227) refers to Alma 33:18-22, which indicates this act was a symbol or type of the coming of the Son of God, who also would be lifted up (crucified and resurrected) in order that his people might live eternally. The latter scripture both clarifies and completes the former and might be marked in the footnote to indicate its importance.

2. Mark scriptural references from modern scriptures.

Another possibility for marking scriptural cross-references would be to mark only those which come from the modern scriptures: Book of Mormon, Doctrine and Covenants, and Pearl of Great Price. Such markings in a different distinctive color for each modern scripture might be justified on the basis that this is the first edition of the Bible to include such cross-references.

9

Marking Footnote Entries Containing Editorial Notes

Some of the footnote entries contain editorial notes not introduced by the capitalized headings GR, HEB, IE, JST, TG, and OR.

For example, Genesis 4:17 refers to Enoch the son of Cain and to the city that was called after his name. Footnote 17b (page 7) pertaining to this scripture notes: "Do not confuse Enoch of Cain's lineage and the city of his name with the Enoch of Seth's lineage and the city (Zion) of his name."

You might want to block such footnotes in a pale color (such as pink).

Footnote entries containing important and informational editorial notes are on the pages listed below. Read and review each of these notes; then decide whether you want to block them in a distinctive color.

8	26	52	76
9	29	56	84
21	44	73	86
23	46(2)	75(2)	93

177	471	874	1161
190	479	875(3)	1166(2)
199	486	877(2)	1187
286	487	878(3)	1189
316	491	880	1192
322	552(2)	882	1193
346	597	886	1197
350	605	890	1198
356	650(3)	892(2)	1216
366	651	917	1227
380	652	941	1241
383	653	1028	1269
384	658	1051	1272
402	744	1055	1328
418	819	1066	1331
422	839	1068(2)	1332
427	858	1080	1342
432	864	1101	1378
440	865	1102	1416
461	869	1104(2)	1460
462	872(2)	1109(2)	1564
465	873	1112	1576(2)

10

Marking Topical Guide Entries

Traditional methods of marking the scriptures have usually included "link referencing" or "chain referencing." Briefly stated, this system of cross-referencing ties or links one scripture to another until all the major scriptures related to that particular subject are linked together in a chain.

This system has proven to be very effective and still has value in marking the text of the scriptures. For example, the account of Jesus calming the waves and the wind is recorded in three of the Gospels: Matthew 8:23-27; Mark 4:36-41; Luke 8:22-25. The footnotes in the new Bible do not lead you from one of these sources directly to the other two. Thus, you might want to link these references together by noting in the margin near each of these references the book, chapter, and verses of the other sources.

The Topical Guide printed in the Appendix of the Bible already accomplishes for the reader much of what was formerly achieved through a link or chain referencing system. Physically, at least, the major scriptures related to a particular subject often have been brought together. However, publication of the Topical Guide opens up many new and creative possibilities for marking the scriptures. Now that related scriptures have been brought together physically, they can quickly, effectively, and efficiently be organized and reorganized into different relationships.

Organization of Topical Guide Entries

So that you can become acquainted with the various components of TG entries, let's examine various types feature by feature. You will note the following:

1. TG (Topical Guide) entries are listed alphabetically.

2. TG entry headings are printed in bold type and are usually capitalized. The only entries not capitalized are *god* and *lord*, which both begin with lowercase letters to distinguish them from two other entries spelled the same way but beginning with capital letters: *God* and *Lord*. The reason for this deviation, of course, is to differentiate when these words are being used in a general sense and when they refer to Deity.

3. TG headings are sometimes followed immediately by information in brackets; this information may indicate whether the word is being used as a verb, noun, etc., or may list a word that might be considered a synonym. (See for example, the entries "Cleave" and "Wax.")

4. TG entry headings are frequently followed by notations in parentheses that serve as cross-references to other sources. If an entry does *not* contain scriptural references, the parenthetical notation usually will be introduced by the word *see*. If an entry contains scriptural references, the parenthetical notation will usually be introduced by the words *see also*. (Some exceptions are "Corn" [p. 76], "Fast, Fasting" [p. 139], "Lord, Spirit of" [p. 298], "Rainbow" [p. 407,], "Spiritually" [p. 495], and "Wrong" [p. 594].)

5. TG headings (and parenthetical notations, when applicable) are usually followed by a series of selected scriptural references pertaining to that particular topic. These references include book, chapter, and verse. The books are listed in the order in which they appear in their respective scriptures, with books from the Old Testament being listed first, followed in order by books from the New Testament, Book of Mormon, Doctrine and Covenants, and Pearl of Great Price.

Clothe (*see also* Array; Gird)

Isa. 61: 10 he hath *c.* me with the gar-ments of salvation; **Dan.** 5: 29 *c.* Daniel with scarlet; **Matt.** 25: 36 Naked, and ye *c.* me; **Mark** 15: 17 *c.* him with purple; **2 Cor.** 5: 2 *c.* upon with our house which is from heaven; **1 Pet.** 5: 5 be *c.* with humility; **Rev.** 11: 3 *c.* in sackcloth; 12: 1 woman *c.* with the sun; 19: 13 *c.* with a vesture dipped in blood; **2 Ne.** 9: 14 *c.* with purity; **3 Ne.** 11: 8 *c.* in a white robe; **D&C** 45: 44 *c.* with power and great glory; 65: 5 *c.* in the brightness of his glory; 88: 125 *c.* yourselves with the bond of charity; 138: 43 bones...*c.* upon with flesh; **Moses** 4: 27 make coats of skins, and *c.* them.

Old Testament

New Testament

Book of Mormon

Doctrine and Covenants

Pearl of Great Price

6. Titles of books in the scriptures are printed in boldface type the *first* time the book is quoted and in every TG entry as a major cross-reference (outside parentheses). An exception to this principle concerns the very first major scriptural reference after each entry heading. The book of this scripture is *not* printed in bold type, as it was felt that it might be confused with the bold-face heading. An ambitious marking project would be to block or circle the title of the first book of scripture quoted in each entry so that this title would be somewhat equal to the titles of the books of scripture printed in boldface type. This book title will always be immediately under and flush left with the TG entry heading.

Arise, Arose (*see also* Rise)

Isa. 26: 19 together with my dead body shall they *a.*; 60: 1 A., shine, for thy light is come; **Amos** 7: 2 by whom shall Jacob *a.*; **Mal.** 4: 2 *a.* with healing in his wings;

Banner

Ps 20: 5 in the name of our God we will set up our *b.*; 60: 4 Thou hast given a *b.* to them that fear thee; **Isa.** 13: 2 Lift ye up a *b.* upon the high mountain.

Restrain (*see also* Hinder; Withhold)
1 Sam. 3: 13 his sons made themselves vile, and he *r*. them not; **Isa.** 63: 15 thy mercies toward me? are they *r*.; **Acts** 14: 18 these sayings scarce *r*. they the people; **2 Ne.** 1: 26 truth, according to that which is in God, which he could not *r*.; **Ether** 12: 2 he could not be *r*. because of the Spirit; **D&C** 134: 4 civil magistrate should *r*. crime.

An even more ambitious marking and coloring project would be to circle in different colors the first major reference from *each* of the standard works. This procedure would help you to determine quickly whether or not a particular standard work (Old Testament, New Testament, Book of Mormon, Doctrine and Covenants, Pearl of Great Price) is represented in the cross-references of an entry.

Marking the Contents of the TG Entries

The extent of your creativity and imagination will be the only limiting factor on how you mark and color the contents of the TG entries. Now that related scriptures are printed together on hundreds of topics, many new, creative, and significant methods for marking the scriptures are possible.

I hesitate to provide even one example for fear it might limit or structure your thinking on how you might mark and/or color the various TG entries. However, to help you start thinking of various possibilities, let's look at the headings associated with baptism, the first basic ordinance of the gospel: Baptism; Baptism, Essential; Baptism, Immersion; Baptism, Qualifications for; Baptism for the Dead (pages 22-23 of the Appendix). Because these five headings are concerned with a common basic subject, you might want to box them in a common color to set them apart from the other headings on those pages.

Now let's list *your* main interests concerning the ordinance of baptism. We'll assume they include the following:

1. How long has baptism been performed on the earth?
2. What are the major purposes of baptism by water?

3. Do the scriptures definitely teach baptism must be by immersion?

4. How clearly do the scriptures indicate priesthood authority is necessary for baptism?

You might mark scriptures pertaining to your first interest (How long has baptism been performed on the earth?) by identifying, numbering, and circling the scriptures indicating *chronologically* when baptism was taught on the earth.

Next, you might help set apart scriptures pertaining to your second interest (What are the major purposes of baptism by water?) by writing "Purposes of baptism by water" in the left margin with a colored pencil (yellow, to remind you of a fresh, new life and of the light of the Holy Ghost?). Then read all the scriptural references under all five headings, identify which ones are concerned with the purposes of baptism, and underline those scriptural references and their key words with the same colored pencil.

Scriptural references pertaining to your third interest (Do the scriptures definitely teach baptism must be by immersion?) have already been compiled under the topic *Baptism, Immersion.* Now all you need to do is identify the scriptures you feel are most important in teaching this concept; then underline those references (in blue, to remind you of water?).

Scriptural references pertaining to your fourth interest (How clearly do the scriptures indicate priesthood authority is necessary for baptism?) might be scattered throughout the five entries. Again, read each reference, identify those that have to do with the authority necessary to baptize, and lightly shade them (in purple, to remind you of the "royal" priesthood and also to indicate how rare and precious the scriptures are on this subject?).

11

Marking Bible Dictionary Entries

Usually you will use the Bible Dictionary only when you want clarification or help with a particular word or term. However, several words and terms in the Bible Dictionary do not even appear in the Bible (i.e. *paraclete*), and other words might not be readily associated with a Bible dictionary (i.e. *Tell el-Amarna Letters*).

Thus, at least once you might want to read on a systematic basis the contents of all Bible Dictionary entries, from the first word (*Aaron*, page 599) through the last word (*Zipporah*, page 793). As you read each of these entries, mark the headings and the contents in the same colors and patterns you used in marking the King James text.

Following are additional suggestions for marking the headings and contents of Bible Dictionary entries.

Inserting Running Heads

Since entries in the Bible Dictionary are listed alphabetically, it was not felt necessary to include running heads in order for a person to find readily any particular entry. However, a few pages have no new entries on them. (As examples, see pages 616, 634, 636-45, 673, 683, 685-96, 757-58, 766, 779.) On such pages you may want to write on the top of the page the word or term being discussed on that particular page.

You might even want to include a running head on *each* page of the dictionary. If so, on the top of each left page, write above the printed word *Bible* the topic being discussed on the *first* line of that page. On the top of each right page, write above the printed word *Bible* the topic being discussed on the *last* line of that page.

Adding Headings and Notes

It is impossible to list in a Bible Dictionary consisting of only 195 pages every word or term that might be defined or explained. You also might find that the wording selected for a particular heading does not lead you to that particular subject. Thus you might want to add your own words or terms in the appropriate alphabetical places. You could then either cross-reference the new heading to an existing heading or could define or explain the new heading more fully in the margins of that particular page.

For example, the three-page entry entitled *Quotations* (pages 756-59) has a very interesting detailed list of Old Testament quotations included in New Testament texts. However, many people might not think to look for this material under the title "Quotations." Thus, you might want to write in the title "Old Testament Quotations in New Testament Texts" in the appropriate alphabetical space on page 739.

An example of where you might want to add considerable material (rather than just a heading) is found under the title "Sermon on the Mount" (pages 771-72). This entry is naturally concerned primarily with the Sermon on the Mount as recorded in Matthew 5:1-7:29. However, the entry also includes the note: "The Sermon in Matthew is greatly clarified by the JST, and a similar sermon recorded in 3 Ne. 12-14. These sources reveal that certain plain and precious information has not survived in the KJV account."

You might want to write in the margins (top, bottom, and/or sides) of pages 771 and 772 some of the important clarifications of the Sermon on the Mount provided by the Joseph Smith Translation and the Book of Mormon. For example, these other accounts make it abundantly clear that the beatitudes do not automatically apply to every person in the world, but apply only to those who are willing to go down into the depths of humility, be baptized, and receive the gift of the Holy Ghost. This clarification changes the entire concept of the beatitudes. A person is not blessed simply because he mourns. But *if* he is called upon to mourn, *then* he is blessed *if* he comes down into the depths of humility, is baptized, and receives the Holy Ghost. Essentially the same idea could be expressed by stating that *if* a person has already gone down into the depths of humility, been baptized, and received the gift of the Holy Ghost, *then* he will be blessed when he is called upon to mourn.

An appropriate brief notation (perhaps "Beatitudes apply only to believers") in the margin of page 772 could remind you of this valuable contribution from Latter-day Saint sources to a widely quoted biblical text.

Marking Hebrew and Greek Derivations

Often the dictionary entries include a Hebrew or Greek word or the Hebrew or Greek meaning of the word or term being defined. Hebrew meanings or explanations might be boxed or underlined in blue, and Greek meanings in green to set them apart from other words on the page.

Marking the Headings of Bible Dictionary Entries

Following are five suggestions for marking headings of Bible Dictionary entries.

1. *Mark headings of entries containing significant LDS materials.*

Several entries in the dictionary include significant amounts of LDS materials. These headings deserve to be distinctively marked and might include the following:

Aaronic Priesthood	Atonement	Death
Abraham		Degrees of Glory
Abraham, Covenant of	Baptism	Devil
Angels		Dispensations
Anoint	Christ, Name of	
Apostle	Confirmation	Eden, Garden of

48

Elder
Election
Elias
Enoch
Ephraim
Ephraim, Stick of
Esaias
Evangelist

Faith
Fall of Adam
Family
Fasting
Firstborn
Flesh

Gabriel
Genealogy
God

Heaven
Hell
High Priest
Holy Ghost

Isaiah

Jehovah
Jeremias or Jeremy
Jethro

John the Baptist
John
Joseph (Son of Rachel)
Joseph Smith Translation
Judah, Stick of

Kingdom of Heaven or
    Kingdom of God
Knowledge

Law of Moses
Laying on of hands
Light of Christ
Lord's Day
Lord's prayer
Lost books

Malachi
Marriage
Melchizedek
Melchizedek Priesthood
Methuselah
Ministry
Miracles
Moses

Noah

Paradise
Patriarch
Peter

Prayer
Prophet

Repentance
Restitution; Restoration
Resurrection
Revelation

Sabbath
Sacrifices
Saint
Scripture
Seed of Abraham
Seer
Serpent, Brazen
Son of God
Son of Man
Spirit
Spirit, the Holy

Temple
Tithe
Transfiguration, Mount of

Urim and Thummim

War in Heaven
Writing

Zedekiah
Zion

2. *Mark headings of entries providing background information on books of the Bible.*

The foreword to the Bible Dictionary section indicates "A short account is given of each of the books of the Bible." Although the Bible Dictionary does indeed provide helpful background information on each of the sixty-six books of the Bible, these books are not always discussed under their own titles. For example, all the epistles of Paul are listed and discussed under the general title "Pauline Epistles" (pages 743-48) rather than under the titles of the individual books.

The sixty-six books of the Bible are listed here *in the order* and *under the heading* they are discussed in the Bible Dictionary. This listing should help you to identify and mark the headings where these books are discussed.

Acts of the Apostles, p. 603
Amos, p. 607
Chronicles, p. 635
    (two books discussed)
Daniel, Book of, p. 653
Deuteronomy, p. 656
Ecclesiastes, p. 659
Esther, Book of, p. 667
Exodus, Book of, p. 668
Ezekiel, p. 668
Ezra, p. 669
Genesis, p. 678
Habakkuk, p. 697
Haggai, p. 698
Hosea, p. 705
Isaiah, p. 707
James, Epistle of, p. 709
Jeremiah, p. 711
Job, Book of, p. 713
Joel, p. 714
John, Epistles of, p. 715
    (three books discussed)
John, Gospel of, p. 715
Jonah, p. 716
Joshua, Book of, p. 718
Jude, Epistle of, p. 719
Judges, Book of, p. 719
Kings, Books of, p. 721
    (two books discussed)
Lamentations, Book of, p. 722
Leviticus, p. 724
Luke, p. 726
Malachi, p. 728
Mark, p. 728

Matthew, p. 729
Micah, p. 731
Nahum, p. 736
Nehemiah, p. 738
Numbers, p. 739
Obadiah, p. 739
Pauline Epistles, pp. 743-48
    (major heading; not a separate book)
    Epistles to the Thessalonians, p. 743
        (two books discussed)
    Epistles to the Corinthians, pp. 743-44
        (two books discussed)
    Epistle to the Galatians, pp. 744-45
    Epistle to the Romans, p. 745
    Epistle to the Philippians, pp. 745-46
    Epistle to the Colossians, p. 746
    Epistle to the Ephesians, p. 746
    Epistle to Philemon, p. 746
    Epistle to the Hebrews, pp. 746-47
    1 Timothy, p. 747
    Epistle to Titus, pp. 747-48
    2 Timothy, p. 748
Peter, Epistles of, pp. 749-50
    (two books discussed)
Proverbs, Book of, p. 754
Psalms, pp. 754-55
Revelation of John, pp. 762-63
Ruth, p. 764
Samuel, Books of, p. 769
    (two books discussed)
Song of Solomon, p. 776
Zechariah, p. 791
Zephaniah, p. 792

3. *Mark headings that might not appear in the Bible but whose entries treat subjects important to an understanding of the Bible.*

The Bible Dictionary contains entries dealing with subjects important to the Bible but with titles that might not be thought of readily by the average student of the Bible. In fact, many of these words or terms do not even appear in the Bible. To emphasize their importance and assist in identification, the headings of such entries, including the following, might be distinctively marked. Read each entry to make certain you feel it should be marked; you might also cross-reference it to another entry in the dictionary or to a specific biblical passage.

Agriculture
Annunciation
Architecture

Calendar
Canon
Church
Clothing
Codex
Communion

Dead Sea Scrolls
Diaspora
Dispersion

Education
Essenes
Epicureans

Furniture

Hagiographa
Hasidaeans
Hasmonaean
Hellenists
Hezekiah's Tunnel
House

Inheritance
Italics

Joseph Smith Translation

Knowledge
Kosher

Leviathan
Levirate Marriage
Lost books

Maccabees
Masoretic Text
Mines
Moabite Stone
Money
Music
Mystery

Names of Persons
New Moon

Paraclete
Pentateuch
Phylacteries
Pseudepigrapha

Punishments
Purification

Quotations (from the
    Old Testament found
    in the New Testament)

Ras Shamrah Tablets
Roman Empire

Sabbath Day's Journey
Sabbatical Year
Scroll
Septuagint
Ship, Shipping
Stories
Symbolism

Talmud
Tell el-Amarna Letters
Torah

Vulgate

Watches
Weaving
Writing

4. *Mark headings consisting of words with meanings that have changed or may be confused with similar words.*

Many words in the Bible are confusing to the average reader because the meanings today are not the same as anciently. Meanings of some of these words changed during the period of writing and compiling the Bible itself, while the meanings of other words have changed drastically since the publication of the King James Text in 1611. Still other words are either obsolete or archaic or

51

might be understood to mean something other than what they actually do mean.

Several of these difficult or confusing words are used as headings of Bible Dictionary entries. Review the contents of the following dictionary entries and determine whether or not these headings should be distinctively marked:

Admiration	Helve	Peculiar
	Hough	Pit
Baal (see also		Presently
Names of Persons)	Isles	
Bittern		Recorder
Bottles	Kine	Reins
By and by	Knop	Rod (has several
		meanings)
Carbuncle	Lees	
Carriage		Spikenard
Caul	Mallows	Suffer(ed)
Censer	Mandrake	
College	Mean	Tempt (has several
Coney	Meat	meanings)
Coulter	Meet	Tire
	Mystery	Turtle
Fear		
Fullers	Nazarite	Watches
		Wimple
Helps	Occupy	

5. *Mark headings of entries containing extensive description on that particular subject.*

The Bible Dictionary contains several entries that contain such extensive helpful information that they are really treatises on the subject rather than simply dictionary definitions. Such titles include the following and might be prominently marked:

Aaronic Priesthood	Circumcision
Abraham, Covenant of	Egypt
Angels	Fasts
Apocrypha (pp. 610-11)	Feasts
Ark of the Covenant	Gospels (Harmony of the Gospels) (pp. 682-96)
Assyria and Babylonia	Jerusalem
Bible (pp. 622-25)	Joseph Smith Translation
Chronology (pp. 635-45)	Maccabees

Palestine	Scribe
Parables	Synagogue
Priests	Tabernacle
Sadducees	Urim and Thummim
Samaritans	Wilderness of the Exodus
Sanhedrin	

Marking the Contents of Bible Dictionary Entries

The contents of Bible Dictionary entries should be marked in the same colors and patterns as the King James text. In addition, you might want to consider the following possibilities of marking the contents of these entries.

1. *Mark references from modern scriptures and the Joseph Smith Translation.*

Entries in the Bible Dictionary are frequently strengthened by the inclusion of references from the Joseph Smith Translation of the Bible, Book of Mormon, Doctrine and Covenants, and Pearl of Great Price. Marking references from each of these sources in a different color would assist in finding such references and would also emphasize important contributions of modern scriptures in understanding concepts and doctrines taught in the Bible.

2. *Mark references from the* History of the Church.

The footnotes and the Topical Guide do not contain any references from the seven-volume *History of the Church* (HC). The Bible Dictionary, however, contains several references to helpful and informational sections of the HC. These deserve to be prominently marked in a distinctive color.

The following list identifies locations of HC references and will help you locate and mark them:

Location and Extent of HC References

Page Number	Dictionary Entry	Extent of HC Reference
600	Abel	2:15-16
604	Adam	3:385-87; 4:207-8
608	Angels	3:386; 3:392
624	Bible Preservation of the Text of the New Testament	1:245; 6:57

648	Comforter	3:381
649	Confirmation	5:499
657	Dispensations	3:386-89; 4:208-9
658	Dove, Sign of	5:261
668	Evangelist	3:381
676	Gabriel	3:386
689	Harmony of the Gospels (chart)	2:264-72
693	Harmony of the Gospels (chart)	5:336
721	Knowledge	4:588
735	Moses	3:387
739	Noah	3:386 (listed twice)
742	Paradise	5:424-25
750	Peter, Epistles of	5:392
762	Revelation	6:58
762	Revelation of John	5:342
763	Revelation of John	5:343
786	Transfiguration, Mount of	3:387; 1:283
793	Zion	6:318-19

Marking Specialized Entries

Several entries in the Bible Dictionary are concerned with special subjects and thus might well be marked in a special way. Following are examples of such special entries:

1. *Chronological Tables.*

The chronological tables (pages 635-45) provide a wealth of valuable information. Read and review this material carefully; then mark and annotate to draw attention to items of special interest. For example, it might be helpful to underline in color the names of the prophets (listed in column 4, "Internal History") so you can readily identify which prophets were prophesying in the days of which kings.

Note also in the section covering the period of the divided kingdoms of Israel (pages 637-39) the differences between the dates in the first column (B.C.), which follow the books of Kings and Chronicles and the dates in the third column (Rev. Chr. for Revised Chronology), which are derived from nonbiblical sources. Down to the time of Ahaz, king of Judah, the Revised Chronology dates are consistently later than the dates obtained from Kings and Chronicles.

2. Harmony of the Gospels.

The Bible Dictionary entry entitled "Harmony of the Gospels" (pp. 684-96) contains a wealth of information concerning the life and teachings of Jesus Christ. Note particularly the scriptural references listed under "Latter-day Revelation" in the far right column of each page.

You might want to underline in red all the items pertaining to the "Event" in the left column where "Latter-day Revelation" in the right column adds considerable information. As examples, note the helpful information from "Latter-day Revelation" concerning the following "Events":

Page 684	Birth of Jesus
	Naming of Jesus
Page 685	John's prophetic ministry
	Baptism of Jesus
	Temptation of Jesus
	John the Baptist's testimony
Page 686	Twelve called and ordained
	Sermon on the Mount
Page 687	Salt of the earth
	Adultery, lust
Page 688	Healing in the evening
	John's disciples ask . . .
Page 689	Pharisees asked for a sign
	Parable . . . tares
Page 691	Seventy appointed
	Jesus' promise of rest
Page 692	Twelve to judge the tribes of Israel
Page 693	Discourse: Sign of second coming
Page 694	Parable: Ten Virgins
	Peter's protest
Page 695	Jesus' suffering and prayer
	The Crucifixion
Page 696	First day: Earthquake, angels open tomb
	Testimony about John

3. Names of Persons.

The entry *Names of Persons* in the Bible Dictionary provides helpful information on the way Hebrew names are composed and the meaning of some of the basic roots. The basic roots might be marked in a distinctive color both as they are explained and then as they appear in the actual names.

4. Quotations.

Under the entry *Quotations*, the Bible Dictionary includes a list of some Old Testament passages quoted or paraphrased by New Testament writers. This three-page entry can be marked in several ways to help the reader remember important aspects. For example, a simple counting of separate Old Testament passages included in the list indicates that the four Old Testament books quoted most frequently by New Testament writers are Psalms, Isaiah, Exodus, and Deuteronomy. You might want to distinctively mark the titles of these four books. Also you might want to number all of the Old Testament books listed in the order of frequency in which they are quoted by the New Testament authors.

5. Pauline Epistles.

The entry *Pauline Epistles* in the Bible Dictionary covers over five pages (pages 743-48) and includes a brief analysis of each of the epistles, organized according to the traditional dates the epistles were originally written. These offer several possibilities for creative marking, such as: (a) place where letter was written; (b) essential contents of epistles; (c) dates of writing; (d) groupings of epistles (note that they are already organized into four major groupings).

6. Weights and Measures.

The entry *Weights and Measures* in the Bible Dictionary includes very helpful information that should be identified and distinctively marked.

12

Marking the Joseph Smith Translation Section

The following explanation appears on the page opposite Genesis, chapter 1: *"Joseph Smith Translation:* Excerpts from the Prophet Joseph Smith's translation of the Bible. Short excerpts are provided in the footnotes [abbreviated JST]; longer excerpts are provided in the Appendix. Italic type in these JST excerpts is used for words not found in the King James Version."

The Appendix section titled "Joseph Smith Translation" (pages 795-813) contains the "excerpts too lengthy for inclusion in footnotes." In the main, you will want to use the same systems of marking and coloring this section as you used for the King James text. For example, if you have decided to underline in blue the King James references to the house of Israel, then you should underline in blue similar references in the Joseph Smith Translation.

The JST excerpts offer special opportunities for creative marking and coloring, including the following:

1. *Emphasize the significant contributions of the JST text.*

If the JST contribution consists of only a word here and

there, you might want to shade lightly (in a color of your choosing) the words that are italicized. If the contribution is too lengthy and continuous, you might indicate its importance (in the same color) by vertical lining in the margin.

2. *Add or note additional JST contributions to your KJV text.*

It was not possible to include all the worthwhile JST references in the new edition of the Bible, either as footnotes or in the special Appendix section. Nor is it possible to include or even list all of them in a brief publication. However, Appendix C of this publication includes a listing of several significant JST excerpts not included in the new Bible edition. Some of these are quoted in some detail with corresponding quotations from the KJV. Other JST references are listed simply by book, chapter, and verse, with corresponding information from the KJV. It is suggested that you read thoroughly all the information and suggestions in Appendix C. Then decide which materials you feel are important enough to note in your copy of the Bible.

3. *Add information on KJV references to the JST excerpts in the Appendix.*

The following note appears on page 813 of the Appendix at the very end of the Joseph Smith Translation section: "Note the changed sequence of verses in the JST." This brief notation informs you the JST verse references are not always the same as the KJV verse references. However, it does not help you discover what those changes are.

It is helpful and frequently very informative to compare the corresponding contents of these two important Bible translations. This is relatively easy to do if you are reading from the KJV text because the superscripts there will lead you to the JST excerpts in the footnotes and in the Appendix. However, it is more difficult to make the comparison if you are reading from the JST excerpts in the Appendix because the JST verse numbers are frequently different from the verse numbers of corresponding material in the KJV. For example, the first JST excerpt in the Appendix is Genesis 9:4-6 (page 797). However, the corresponding material in the KJV is in Genesis 8:20-24 (page 12).

The information in the list that follows will help you make these comparisons directly from the JST excerpts in the Appendix. The references of the JST excerpts are listed by book, chapter, and verse. The numbers of the pages containing the corresponding materials in the KJV are then listed in parentheses.

Gen. 9:4-6 (12)	Matt. 7:4-8 (1197)	Luke 21:24-25 (1316)
Gen. 9:10-14 (13)	Matt. 7:9-11 (1197)	Luke 24:2-4 (1322)
Gen. 9:21-25 (13)	Matt. 7:12-17 (1197)	John 1:1-34 (1324)
Gen. 14:25-40 (20)	Matt. 9:18-21 (1201)	John 4:1-4 (1330)
Gen. 15:9-12 (21)	Matt. 11:13-15 (1205)	John 6:44 (1336)
Gen. 17:3-7 (22)	Matt. 12:37-38 (1208)	John 13:8-10 (1351)
Gen. 17:11-12 (23)	Matt. 13:39-44 (1211)	Acts 22:29-30 (1406)
Gen. 19:9-15 (26)	Matt. 16:27-29 (1216)	Rom. 3:5-8 (1419)
Gen. 21:31-32 (30)	Matt. 17:10-14 (1217)	Rom. 4:2-5 (1420)
Gen. 48:5-11 (74)	Matt. 21:47-56 (1225)	Rom. 7:5-27 (1424)
Gen. 50:24-38 (78)	Matt. 26:24-25 (1235)	Rom. 8:29-30 (1427)
Ex. 4:24-27 (84)	Mark 2:26-27 (1245)	Rom. 13:6-7 (1433)
Ex. 32:14 (130)	Mark 3:21-25 (1246)	1 Cor. 7:29-33 (1446)
Ex. 33:20 (133)	Mark 7:10-12 (1253)	Gal. 3:19-20 (1476)
Ex. 34:1-2 (133)	Mark 8:37-38 (1255)	Col. 2:21-22 (1495)
1 Chr. 21:15 (575)	Mark 8:42-43 (1255)	2 Thes. 2:7-9 (1504)
Ps. 11:1-5 (719)	Mark 9:40-48 (1258)	1 Tim. 2:4 (1507)
Ps. 14:1-7 (720)	Mark 14:20-25 (1266)	1 Tim. 3:15-16 (1508)
Ps. 24:7-10 (728)	Mark 14:36-38 (1267)	1 Tim. 6:15-16 (1512)
Isa. 29:1-8 (895)	Mark 16:3-6 (1270)	Heb. 4:3 (1524)
Isa. 42:19-23 (912)	Luke 3:4-11 (1277)	Heb. 6:3-10 (1526)
Matt. 3:4-6 (1188)	Luke 3:19-20 (1278)	Heb. 7:3 (1527)
Matt. 3:24-26 (1189)	Luke 6:29-30 (1284)	Heb. 7:19-21 (1527)
Matt. 3:34-36 (1190)	Luke 9:24-25 (1291)	Heb. 7:25-26 (1528)
Matt. 3:38-40 (1190)	Luke 12:9-12 (1299)	James 2:14-21 (1540)
Matt. 3:43-46 (1190)	Luke 12:41-57 (1300)	Rev. 1:1-8 (1565)
Matt. 5:21 (1193)	Luke 14:35-37 (1304)	Rev. 2:26-27 (1568)
Matt. 6:25-27 (1196)	Luke 16:16-23 (1307)	Rev. 12:1-17 (1576)
	Luke 17:36-40 (1309)	

You might want to write these page numbers in your copy of the Appendix next to the appropriate JST references as indicated in the following examples:

ISAIAH 42: 19–23 *P. 912*

19 *For I will send my servant unto you who are blind; yea, a messenger to open the eyes of the blind, and unstop the ears of the deaf;*

20 *And they shall be made perfect notwithstanding their blindness, if they will hearken unto the messenger, the Lord's servant.*

21 *Thou art a people,* seeing many things, but thou observest not; opening the ears

MATTHEW 11: 13–15 *p. 1205*

13 *But the days will come, when the violent shall have no power* ; for all the prophets and the law prophesied *that it should be thus* until John.

14 *Yea, as many as have prophesied have foretold of these days.*

15 And if ye will receive it, *verily, he was the* Elias, *who* was for to come *and prepare all things.*

The insertion of these page numbers will be helpful as you compare the contents of the Joseph Smith Translation with the King James Version.

13

Marking the Gazetteer

The first two sentences of instructions under the Gazetteer on page 817 are as follows: "In the list of references below, the letters and numbers in bold type refer to the grid squares in which place names are found on the maps in the map section that follows. Numbers in ordinary type refer to the numbers of the maps in which the place names occur in the indicated grid positions."

Many people will be surprised (and perhaps even confused) to find the map number is not listed *before* the letters and numbers indicating the grid squares of that particular map. After all, you must know the map with which you are working before the grid squares have any significance. To emphasize the importance of the map numbers in each entry, they could be marked with a light color.

The last sentence of instructions under Gazetteer indicates "References marked with an asterisk appear only in the large-print Bible." This sentence might be crossed out and disregarded because all the places marked with an asterisk *do* appear in the regular-print Bibles. Some differences do exist between the maps in the regular-print Bibles and in the large-print Bibles, but most of those differences are not major and they do not pertain to the entries marked with an asterisk.

Other possibilities for marking Gazetteer entries include the following:

1. *Listing places under different headings.* As might be expected, the same geographical place or area is often known by different names in different periods of history. The gazetteer helpfully solves this problem by listing the place alphabetically under its different titles, with the other titles placed in parentheses. Thus:

Acco (Ptolemais) on page 817
Ptolemais (Acco) on page 824

However, the listings in the Gazetteer are not always one hundred percent consistent in listing *all* the possible titles in parentheses, especially when three or more titles are involved. To help complete an otherwise excellent Gazetteer, you might want to write in your Bible the italicized words listed in the following entries:

Alashuja (Cyprus, *Kittim*) *island*
Arabs, people (*Aribi*)
Ararat (Urartu) *region*
Asphaltitus, Lake (*Dead Sea, Salt Sea*)
Eastern Sea (*Lower Sea, Persian Gulf*) (Add entire entry just before Ebal, Mount, on page 820)
Great (Mediterranean, Upper, *Western*) Sea
Heliopolis, in Egypt (*On*)
Hittites (*Hatti*), people
Julias (Livias, *Batharamphtha*)
Kittim (*Alashiza, Cyprus*) *island* (Add entire entry just before Kizzuwatna, region, on page 822)
Libias (*Betharamphtha*; Julias) (Note that *Libias* can also be spelled *Livias*)
Nimrud (*Cala*) (Add entire entry just before Nineveh, page 823)
Persian Gulf (*Eastern Sea*, Lower Sea)
Scythopolis (*Beth-shan*) (Note that *Beth-shan* can also be spelled *Beth-shean*)
Susa (*Shushan*)
Syria (*Aram*)
Tell en-Nasbeh (*Mizpah*) (Add entire entry just before Tell Halaf on page 825)
Upper (Great, *Mediterranean*, Western) Sea
Western (*Great, Mediterranean, Upper*) Sea (Add entire entry just before Xanthus on page 826)

2. *Tying together entries with identical first words.* Several entries in the Gazetteer begin with identical words. You might want to tie them together as indicated so you will be certain to look at both entries when you are looking for a particular location:

┌─Emmaus (Nicopolis)
└─Emmaus

Following is a list of Gazetteer entries where the same word is used at least twice to begin consecutive entries:

Abila, Aijalon, Alexandria, Antioch, Aphek, Apollonia, Aram, Ararat, Arbela, Babylonia, Beth-horon, Beth-shemesh, Bithynia, Caesarea, Chinnereth, Crete, Cyprus, Egypt, Emmaus, Gadara, Galilee, Gath, Gerar, Heliopolis, Herod, Israel, Judah, Judea, Kadesh, Laodicea, Lower, Lydia, Moab, Neapolis, Nicopolis, Nile, North, Persian, Philadelphia, Philistia, Samaria, Seleucia, Sin, Sinai, Succoth, Tell, Temple, Tepe, Tyre, and Upper.

3. *Marking Old Testament and New Testament places.*

Another possibility for marking the entries in the Gazetteer would be to encircle in one color (blue?) those places primarily associated with the Old Testament, and encircle in another color (green?) the important New Testament places. Nazareth, for example, is not mentioned in the Old Testament but is a prominent New Testament place name, so it would be encircled in the color you select for the New Testament. Following are lists of major place names you might want to mark:

Old Testament Place Names
Ai; Amman (Rabbah); Ammon; Arad; Ararat, Mount; Ashdod; Ashkelon; Assyria.
Babylon; Babylonia; Beer-sheba; Bethel; Beth-shan; Beth-shemesh.
Dan (Laish); Dead (Salt) Sea; Dothan.
Ebal, Mount; Egypt (all entries but Roman province); Ekron; En-gedi; Ezion-geber.
Gath; Gaza; Gerizim, Mount; Gibeon; Gilboa, Mount.
Haran; Hazor; Hebron.
Jabbok, river; Jezreel, Valley of.
Kadesh-barnea; Kiriath-jearim; Kishon, river.
Lachish; Lod.
Megiddo; Mizpah (Tell en-Nasbeh); Moab.
Nebo, Mount; Nineveh.
Penuel; Persia; Philistines, people.
Rabbah (Amman); Ramah; Ramoth-gilead; Red Sea.

Salt (Dead) Sea; Shechem; Shur, Wilderness of; Sinai.
Ur.
Ziklag; Zin, Wilderness of.

New Testament Place Names
Antioch (both entries); Arimathea; Athens.
Bethany; Bethesda, Pool of, in Jerusalem.
Caesarea (all five entries); Calvary (Golgotha) in Jerusalem; Capernaum;
    Carthage; Chorazin; Corinth; Crete, Roman Province; Cyprus, in
    Palestine; Cyprus, Roman province.
Emmaus (Nicopolis); Ephesus.
Gadara (both entries); Galilee (all entries); Garden Tomb; Gethsemane, in
    Jerusalem; Golgotha (Calvary), in Jerusalem.
Hinnom Valley, in Jerusalem.
Kidron Valley, in Jerusalem.
Lydda.
Malta.
Nain; Nazareth.
Olives, Mount of.
Pella; Perea; Philippi.
Rome.
Salamis.
Tarsus; Thessalonica; Tiberias; Tyropoeon Valley, in Jerusalem.
Upper room, in Jerusalem.
Water Gate, in Jerusalem.

Place Names in Both the Old Testament and New Testament
    Some place names are prominent in the times of both the Old Testament
and New Testament. You might want to encircle them in one color (blue?) and
shade them in the other color (green?). These places are: Bethlehem; Damascus;
Egypt; Jericho; Jerusalem; Jordan, river; Judea, region; Samaria; Sidon; Syria;
Tabor, Mount; Tyre.

14

Marking the Maps

The twenty-two maps at the end of the Appendix are a valuable addition to this excellent Bible and, in general, should not be marked excessively. In fact, a good principle of marking related to these and other maps would be: do not mark unless necessary for correction or clarification.

However, more marking than usual might be necessary on these maps because in the 1979 edition the maps in the large-print Bible are not the same as the maps in the regular-size Bible, yet both are served by an identical Gazetteer. Unfortunately the different sizes and layouts of the pages in the two editions necessitated the use of different maps, which appear at first glance to be the same but which sometimes differ significantly on closer inspection.

In order to make the two sets of maps as similar as possible and also make them consistent with the Gazetteer entries, at least the following minimum changes should be made. The first set of instructions pertains to marking a large-print edition (6 x 9 inches) of the Bible. The second set of instructions applies to a regular-size (5 x 7¼ inches) edition.

1. *In the large-print edition of the Bible:*

a. The places listed in the center column below do not appear on the indicated maps even though Gazetteer entries indicate they should. Place dots and write in the names of those places on the appropriate maps in your copy of the Bible. To help you locate the places more precisely, corresponding sections of maps from the regular-size edition are reproduced on the right:

Sections of Maps from
Large-print Edition

Sections of Maps from
Regular-size Edition

Map 4
Shittim E3:4

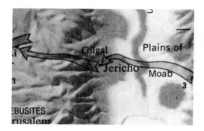

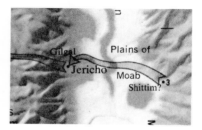

Map 9
Gerar B7:9

Map 10
Black Sea **D7**:10
Byzantium **B1**:10, 12

Map 19
Damascus **D5**:19

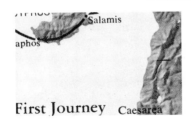

Map 20, 21
Smyrna C2:20, 21

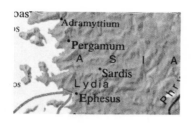

b. On map 10, write the word "Tribute" before the words "to Assyria 671-651 B.C.," which are found just below the large heading E G Y P T in grid B3.

2. *In the regular-size edition of the Bible:*

a. The places listed in the center column below do not appear on the indicated maps of the regular-size Bible, even though the Gazetteer entries indicate they should. Place dots and write in the names of those places on the appropriate maps in your copy of the Bible. To help you locate the places more precisely, corresponding sections of maps from the large-print edition are reproduced on the right:

Sections of Maps from
Regular-size Edition

Sections of Maps from
Large-print Edition

Map 3

Taanach **D2:3**   Zoar **D3:3**

Map 5
Achzib **B3**:5, 6
Ahlab **B2**:5

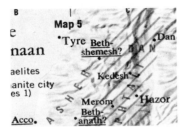
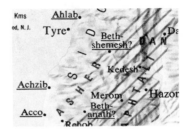

Map 10
Hermopolis **B4**:10

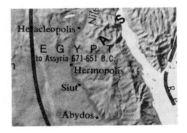

Map 12
Sais **B3**:10, 11, 12
Sippar **C2**:12
Tadmor **C2**:12

Map 14
Paneas **E2**:14

Map 19
Lyconia **C4**:19

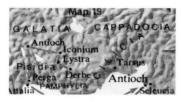

Map 20
Judea, region **E4**:20

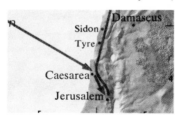
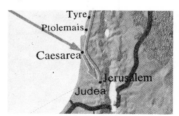

b. On map 1, write just after the line listing the copyright information: Elevations are given in feet.

c. On map 5, write just after the marks in the legend indicating distances: Red titles represent tribes of Israel.

d. On map 8, the following cities are royal cities of Solomon and, according to the information in the legend, should be underlined: Jerusalem (C6); Gezer (B5); Megiddo (B4); and Hazor (C3).

e. On map 17, add the words "of Jesus' day" to the sentence in the legend (E1) that begins: "Probable location of city walls." Also, two lines below the above sentence, add the words "of the Old City of Jerusalem" to the sentence in the legend that begins: "Present-day walls."

Marking the Titles of the Maps

Another possibility for marking the map section of the Appendix would be to underline in color the titles of the maps listed on page 827. The titles of maps concerned primarily with the Old Testament (maps 2-12) could be underlined in blue, and the titles of maps concerned primarily with the New Testament (maps 13-22) could be underlined in green. Note that map 1 can be used extensively with both the Old Testament and the New Testament.

15

Locating Books and Appendix Sections in the Bible

Only the most expensive copies of the new edition of the Bible contain thumb indexing. Yet most Bible readers agree the thumb index provides a method of quick access to specific books. This brief section suggests a simple, inexpensive method for providing ready access to the books of the scriptures that may be nearly as effective as—and, in some instances, even more effective than—the thumb index. This method encourages and explains the development of a possible color-marking system that will enable you to locate quickly all the books of the Bible, as well as major sections of the Appendix.

On the last page of this book, you will note two columns listing the full titles and the approved abbreviations of the 66 biblical books in the order in which they appear in the Bible. The right column lists the 39 books of the Old Testament; the left column lists the 27 books of the New Testament and also headings related to sections of the Appendix.

The layout of the page enables you to *cut out* these columns (on the dotted lines) without losing any of the regular text of the book, and yet leaves an inside margin of the page so as not to weaken the binding of the book. (You may prefer to retype the lists as they appear here.) If you clip the lists directly from the book, it is suggested that you cut out the two columns first vertically (bottom to top) and then horizontally (side to side) along the dotted lines.

1. Glue (or use rubber cement or sticky tape) the column listing the Old Testament books on the front right-hand endsheet (the thick brown or black page connected directly with the front cover of your Bible) so the top of the column is near the *top* edge (just below the curved corner), and flush with the *right* side.

2. Glue (or use rubber cement or sticky tape) the column listing the New Testament books on the back left-hand endsheet (the brown or black page connected directly with the back cover of your Bible) so the bottom of the column is near the *bottom* edge (just above the curved corner) and flush with the *left* side.

In order to provide a ready access system to the books of the Bible and to selected areas of the Appendix, you will then need to mark small colored squares on some of the appropriate pages of the Bible, as indicated in the following sections.

Marking the Books of the Old Testament

1. First, underline the following eight titles on the Old Testament list, using a different color for each title, as in this example:

Leviticus—purple
Joshua—green
1 Kings—yellow
Ezra—brown
Psalms—orange
Isaiah—blue
Ezekiel—red
Micah—black

2. Color small squares of the same colors as these titles along the right-hand side of the column, next to the titles or abbreviations of the designated books. Now mark your Bible so you can quickly find the beginning place of each of the designated books. For example, to mark Leviticus:

1. Take a ruler and note the exact distance from the top of the page containing the columned list to the top of the small colored square next to the title *Leviticus*.

2. Turn to the first right-hand page after the beginning of Leviticus (page 147 of your Bible).

3. Take your ruler again and make a mark at the very right-hand edge of page 147 the same distance from the top of the page as determined in step 1 above; then make a square below the mark in the same color and about the same size as the square next to the title *Leviticus* in the column glued in the front of the Bible.

4. Follow the procedures listed in step 3 above for the next three right-hand pages of the Bible—149, 151, 153.

Now open your Bible to the page containing the glued column listing all the Old Testament books. Bend your Bible slightly (fanning the pages); look along the colored line under Leviticus and you can readily see the exact place where the book of Leviticus begins in the Bible. By placing your thumbnail where the colored purple marks appear at the beginning of Leviticus, you can open your Bible directly to those pages.

Follow the same principles and procedures in marking the remaining Old Testament books underlined in other colors. The pages you should mark (and colors you might use) are as follows:

Joshua (green)—pages 309, 311, 313, 315
1 Kings (yellow)—pages 463, 465, 467, 469
Ezra (brown)—pages 635, 637, 639, 641
Psalms (orange)—pages 715, 717, 719, 721
Isaiah (blue)—pages 861, 863, 865, 867
Ezekiel (red)—pages 1027, 1029, 1031, 1033
Micah (black)—pages 1151, 1153, 1155, 1157

This system of marking will help you to find and quickly turn to the eight Old Testament books you have marked. Now, how do you obtain quick access to the other books?

You will probably find the marking of these eight books is sufficient to find all the other books in the Old Testament. After all, there is no need to mark Genesis, as it is the first book in the Bible and can be located quickly without any marking system. Also, the glued column at the front lists *all* the Old Testament books *in the order* in which they appear. Thus, if you want to read a reference in Daniel, you will note that Daniel appears right after Ezekiel, which was marked in our example in red. Turn to the marking for Ezekiel and open your Bible there; then quickly leaf through the pages until you come to the next book—Daniel.

If you want to mark your Bible so *every* book can be located precisely and quickly, you can do so by following the same principles and procedures as outlined for the eight books discussed above. You may decide to mark the remaining books in a single color (red shows up very well), or you may want to develop your own coloring system with different colors for different books.

Marking the Books of the New Testament

The same principles and essentially the same procedures should be followed in marking the books of the New Testament so you can turn to them quickly. However, you will want to note the following differences.

The glued list of New Testament books is in the *back* of the Bible, so you should color the squares opposite the eight given titles along the *left*-hand margin.

Thus, when you make small square marks of the same colors on the pages of the text to identify the beginning places of the New Testament books, the marks should be on the outside edge of the *left*-hand page.

Following are the titles of the eight New Testament books to be underlined in color, with the pages that might be marked with small squares in the same color:

Matthew (black)—pages 1188, 1190, 1192, 1194
Mark (red)—pages 1242, 1244, 1246, 1248
Luke (blue)—pages 1272, 1274, 1276, 1278
John (yellow)—pages 1324, 1326, 1328, 1330
Acts (brown)—pages 1366, 1368, 1370, 1372
1 Corinthians (orange)—pages 1438, 1440, 1442, 1444
1 Timothy (green)—pages 1506, 1508, 1510, 1512
1 John (purple)—pages 1556, 1558, 1560, 1562

Marking Sections of the Appendix

Quick access can also be obtained to the major sections of the Appendix. The column that lists the 27 books of the New Testament (which might now be glued in the back of your Bible) also lists the following sections of the Appendix (colors that might be used and pages to be marked are also included below):

TG "A" Topical Guide (black)—pages 2, 4, 6, and 8 of the Appendix

TG "H" Topical Guide (red)—pages 196, 198, 200, and 202 of the Appendix

TG "R" Topical Guide (blue)—pages 406, 408, 410, and 412 of the Appendix

BD "A" Bible Dictionary (yellow)—pages 600, 602, 604, and 606 of the Appendix

BD "Chronological Tables" of Bible Dictionary (brown)—pages 636, 638, 640, and 642 of the Appendix

BD "Harmony of the Gospels" of Bible Dictionary (orange)—pages 684, 686, 688, and 690 of the Appendix

JST Joseph Smith Translation (green)—pages 796 (blank), 798, 800, and 802 of the Appendix

Gaz. Gazetteer (purple)—pages 816 (blank), 818, 820, and 822 of the Appendix

By marking these sections and pages, you can gain:

1. Three ready places of access to the Topical Guide: where entries begin with the letters A, H, and R. Inasmuch as the Topical Guide is arranged alphabetically, you can then quickly find entries beginning with other letters.

2. Three ready places of access to the Bible Dictionary: where entries begin with the letter A, and at the special sections headed "Chronological Tables" and "Harmony of the Gospels."

3. One access to the "Joseph Smith Translation" section.

4. One access to the Gazetteer with its accompanying maps.

Once you realize that the sections of the Joseph Smith Translation (pages 797-813) and the Gazetteer (pages 817-26) are located at the end of the Appendix and thus at the back of the volume, you might decide not to mark accesses to these sections. However, space is provided for you on the printed column if you desire to do so.

Appendix A

Initial Listing of Topics Related to the Bible

Following are initial groups of materials related to or taken from the Bible, both Old Testament and New Testament. These include principles, ordinances, ideas, thoughts, truths, concepts, customs, traditions, practices, and beliefs. Other essential materials should be added, and they might all then be arranged into seven or eight groups to form the basis of an effective marking and coloring system (pp. 27-28).

Group 1. The eternal plan of progression—salvation, exaltation, and eternal life. Pre-earthly existence, including the role of foreordination and reasons for the veil of forgetfulness in mortality. Purposes of this mortal probationary period: the nature of physical birth, which is also a death from the pre-earthly existence, and the nature of physical death, which is a rebirth to a spiritual condition. The post-earthly spirit world: conditions there; how it differs from the pre-earthly spirit world; major purposes of this stage of existence. The resurrection, of the just and the unjust. The final judgment: its nature and extent; the things for which we will be judged; relationship of justice and mercy to the final judgment. The three degrees of glory: types and characteristics of people who inherit each degree of glory; nature of celestial glory. Godhood: the goal of perfection, and to become as God is.

Group 2. The life and mission of Jesus Christ, and his relationship to other members of the Godhead. His pre-earthly position as the Firstborn Son of God in the spirit. His foreordination. His role as the pre-earthly Jehovah in the Old Testament. His role as the only Begotten Son of God in the flesh. The prophesied Messiah, including Old Testament prophecies of his coming. His birth in Bethlehem; his brief sojourn in Egypt; the boy of Nazareth and of the temple; the man of Galilee and of Jerusalem. His teachings and his example. His atonement, with emphasis on what occurred in Gethsemane and at Calvary. His relationship to the Father. The Godhead: the nature, characteristics, and "oneness" of each member. Functions of the Holy Ghost, including his role as a testifier for Christ.

Group 3. Definition, nature, and extent of the gospel of Jesus Christ. Meaning of *gospel.* First principles of the gospel: faith in the Lord Jesus Christ; repentance; hope; charity. The next principles and first essential ordinances of the gospel: baptism by immersion for the remission of sins; laying on of hands for the gift of the Holy Ghost. Other ordinances: the sacrament; conferring of priesthood; ordinations to priesthood offices; endowment; celestial marriage; temple ordinances for the living and the dead. Responsibility for teaching the gospel to others; missionary work; characteristics of a good missionary.

Group 4. Definition and nature of the priesthood. Role and functions of priesthood power and authority throughout the centuries. Purpose of the priesthood. Essential differences between priesthood power and authority and priesthood keys. Major offices and groupings in the priesthood. Which Old Testament prophets and leaders held which priesthood. Matters pertaining to conferral of the priesthood and ordaining to priesthood offices. Matters pertaining to Church organization, government, and administration. Covenant and oath of the priesthood. Sacred calling of a priesthood bearer. Priesthood in the various dispensations of the gospel.

Group 5. Principles of revelation and prophecy. Prerequisites to both revelation and prophecy, including the foreknowledge of God and the witnessing function of the Holy Ghost. The means and power by which our Heavenly Father can reveal his mind to his prophets (revelation and the Holy Ghost). Why does the Lord do nothing save he "revealeth his secrets unto his servants and prophets"? Role, function, nature, and characteristics of prophets. Relationship between prophecy and revelation and the scriptures. What the scriptures are and how God reveals them. Responsibility of the prophet in receiving and recording the scriptures. Responsibility of members to read, study, ponder, and live the teachings in the scriptures. How prophecy and revelation tie in to the other gifts of the spirit: healing, speaking in tongues, etc.

Group 6. The origin and history of the house of Israel. Special role of Jacob and his twelve sons. Distinctions between blood Israel, land Israel, and covenant Israel. Story of the Israelites in Egypt. Delivery from Egypt under Moses. Return to the promised land under Joshua. Major events during times of (a) the judges, (b) the united kingdom under Saul, David, and Solomon, and (c) the divided kingdoms of Israel and Judah. The captivity and scattering of the ten tribes. The scattering of the dispersed of Israel (including Lehi and Mulek). The scattering of Judah by the Babylonians; their return under Cyrus of Persia; their later scattering by the Romans. The major aspects of the prophesied gathering of Israel in the last days: the return of Judah to Jerusalem; the gathering of the dispersed of Israel to the church (covenant Israel); the return of the ten lost tribes.

Group 7. Conditions of the last days leading to the millennial reign of Jesus Christ. Calamities to precede the second coming. Wickedness to increase. Great battles at Armageddon and elsewhere. The gatherings to Jerusalem and to Zion; the preparation of the peoples and the temples there. Events directly associated with the second coming of Jesus Christ in power and great glory. Conditions during the millennium.

Group 8. The nature, disposition, and characteristics of mortal, physical man. In what sense(s) is the natural man carnal, devilish, and sensual? Our spiritual relationship to our Heavenly Father, as his sons and daughters. The importance of the family. The role and responsibility of parents. Husband-wife and parent-child relationships.

Group 9. The basic commandments and laws of God. The ten commandments, including keeping the sabbath day holy. Tithing. The law of the fast and of fast offerings. The Word of

Wisdom. The law of sacrifice. The law of carnal commandments. The symbols, types, and observances under the law of Moses that were to point people toward and prepare them for the coming of Jesus Christ.

Group 10. The role and purpose of opposition in life. The devil: his titles, purposes, methods, characteristics, weaknesses. The place of adversity, sickness, pain, disease, death. Reasons for tests and trials. How to develop hope and faith in order to overcome despair and sin. The place of free agency.

Appendix B

Locating the "GR," "HEB," "IE," "OR" Footnotes

Section 1. Location of "GR" Footnotes

Inasmuch as the King James text of the New Testament is taken primarily from Greek texts, the GR footnote entries (alternate translations from the Greek) are very important to an understanding of the New Testament. The first list below indicates the number of GR footnote entries in each of the twenty-seven books of the New Testament (there are no GR footnotes in the Old Testament).

Matt., 190	Eph., 4	Heb., 53
Mark, 47	Philip., 23	James, 25
Luke, 109	Col., 9	1 Pet., 30
John, 28	1 Thes., 24	2 Pet., 15
Acts, 52	2 Thes., 13	1 Jn., 16
Rom., 131	1 Tim., 54	2 Jn., 1
1 Cor. 123	2 Tim., 28	3 Jn., 1
2 Cor., 20	Titus, 24	Jude, 2
Gal., 29	Philem., 5	Rev., 19

The next list identifies *pages* of the Bible containing GR footnote entries (alternate translations from the Greek). Each of the following pages has at least one GR footnote entry; some of the pages have as many as eleven entries (see, for example, p. 1518). This list should be of assistance in marking GR footnotes.

1187-1215	1310-28	1379	1483-85
1217-46	1330	1381-83	1488-1526
1248-52	1332-34	1386	1528-35
1254-58	1337	1390	1537-42
1260	1339	1393	1544-48
1267-68	1342	1395-96	1550-65
1270-78	1345-47	1398	1568-71
1280-87	1349	1400-1403	1574
1289-90	1351-56	1407-64	1577
1292	1360	1466-68	1579
1294-95	1363	1470-71	1581-83
1297-1306	1366-69	1473-79	1588
1308	1371-76	1481	

Section 2. Location of "HEB" Footnotes

Since the Old Testament text in the King James version is taken primarily from earlier Hebrew texts, the HEB footnote entries (alternate translations from the Hebrew) in the Bible are very important to an understanding of the Old Testament text.

The first list below indicates the number of HEB footnotes in each of the thirty-nine books of the Old Testament (only two books of the New Testament — Romans and Hebrews — have HEB footnotes, and they have only one footnote each).

Gen., 70	1 Kgs., 33	Eccl., 5	Obad., 0
Ex., 111	2 Kgs., 7	Song., 0	Jonah, 2
Lev., 102	1 Chr., 2	Isa., 143	Micah, 4
Num., 86	2 Chr., 29	Jer., 78	Nahum, 5
Deut., 165	Ezra, 6	Lam., 0	Hab., 4
Josh., 28	Neh., 2	Ezek., 90	Zeph., 3
Judg., 46	Esth., 2	Dan., 13	Hag., 1
Ruth, 2	Job, 33	Hosea, 13	Zech., 13
1 Sam., 13	Ps., 74	Joel, 6	Mal., 1
2 Sam., 17	Prov., 10	Amos, 5	

The next list identifies *pages* of the Bible containing HEB footnotes. Each of the following pages has at least one HEB footnote entry; some of them have as many as eight entries (see, for example, p. 175). This list should be of assistance in marking HEB footnotes.

Old Testament

1-7	208-11	441	636
10	213-14	445	638
12-17	216-17	448-49	643
19-20	220-22	451	645
22-23	224-29	453	647-48
26-27	231-34	457-58	654
31	237-38	463-64	672
33-35	240	468	675
37	242-43	471-72	680-83
39-42	246-49	477-78	685-89
45-49	251-58	482-84	692-95
54	260-63	487	698-700
56-58	265-99	491	702-3
73	301-14	493	705
75	316-17	495	708
79-81	319-21	498-99	710-12
83-86	328-29	501-2	714-16
88	331-32	505-6	718-19
90-95	334-35	509	721
97-103	344	512	723-26
105-6	346-54	521	731
108-12	356-65	524	733
114	370-71	527	735
116-19	373	546	737-38
121-29	375	559	742
131-36	377-78	561	744
138-40	383-84	587-88	751
142-46	390	591	754
148	393	593-96	756
151	396	600-602	761
153-59	401	604	763
161-67	407	608-9	765-78
169-70	413-15	616-18	782-87
174-88	418	623-24	792-93
195-201	432	627-28	796-97
203	433-34	630	801-2
205-6	436-39	632-33	805

808-11	918-19	993-94	1073
819	923-25	996-99	1075-85
825	927-28	1001-2	1088
829	930-31	1004	1097
832	933-36	1006-12	1099-1101
836	938-39	1014	1113-14
838	941-42	1016-17	1117-20
843	944-46	1019	1123-29
846	948	1027-29	1132-36
848	952-53	1031	1140-42
851	955-57	1035-36	1144-45
856	960-65	1039-40	1149-53
861-67	969	1042-47	1157-61
869-74	971	1049-51	1163-66
876-90	974	1055-56	1169-70
892-93	981-82	1058	1172
895-910	984-85	1060-61	1174-75
913-14	989-91	1064-71	1179-81

New Testament
1429
1522

Section 3. Location of "IE" Footnotes

The following list identifies the pages containing at least one footnote entry (an explanation of idioms and difficult constructions). This list should be helpful in marking the IE footnote entries.

Old Testament

4	80-81	139	198
9	87	141-42	201-2
14-15	89	148	207
21-23	95-96	150-51	212
27	98-99	153	214
30-33	101-2	155	220
36	105-6	163	222
38-41	108-11	165	224
43-45	113	170	226-28
49	115	174-77	232-33
51-52	118	179-81	236
54-56	120	187-88	248-49
72	127-28	193	255-57
77-78	135-37	195	259-62

264	455	751	1011
267	463	755-56	1013
271	470	769-70	1016
276-83	472-73	781	1019
286	475	783-84	1027
288-91	479	787	1030-32
293	481-82	793	1036-37
298	491-92	795	1040-41
305	502	803	1044
308-9	506	806	1053-56
311-12	515	816	1059-60
314-16	523	818	1064
318	542-43	825-26	1067
329	547	828-29	1069
332-33	588	832-33	1071
342	590-91	835-36	1074
350	594	839-40	1084
354	596-98	842	1090
356	600-601	844-45	1093
359	603-6	853-54	1097
362	610-11	856-57	1100-1101
365-67	613	862-77	1105
369-70	615-16	879-89	1107
373	620	892-906	1110
375	622-23	909-21	1112
377-79	625	923-24	1114-15
382	627	929-33	1117-18
384-85	631	935-37	1120
388	634	939-40	1122-27
391	638-39	944-45	1129
393-95	641	948-49	1131-33
398-401	643	952	1139-42
403	645	958-59	1148-49
405	649-51	962	1151-52
409	655	965	1154-55
416	683	969	1158
418	685	972	1163-64
420	691-92	975	1167-68
422-23	726	984	1170
425	729	988	1176
428	731	991	1180-81
434-36	733	1001	
439	740	1004	

New Testament

1188-89	1217	1319	1429-30
1192-93	1219	1322	1436
1195	1226	1355	1443
1205	1231	1377	1456
1209	1239	1386	1458
1212	1280	1413	1572
1215	1301	1416	

Section 4. Location of "OR" Footnotes

The following list identifies pages in the new LDS edition of the Bible containing at least one footnote entry marked OR (alternate words clarifying the meaning of archaic English expressions). This list should be helpful in marking OR footnote entries:

Old Testament

3-5	193-97	353	487-88
7	200-203	357	490
11-15	211	363	492
18-20	213	366-68	495-96
24	217	371-74	498
28	220	378-82	500-501
30-31	222-25	384	504
38	227-30	387-93	510
43	232-34	395	513
46-47	236	398-400	515
50-52	238-41	403	517
74-75	243-51	406	525-26
78-86	257	409	529
88-105	259-61	413-19	535
107-145	264-74	423	539
147	277-83	428	541
149-50	285-94	430-31	563
161-62	296-302	433	565
170	304-8	450	587-94
172-73	310	452	596-97
176	312-14	456	600-601
178	317-31	458-59	603
182	333	463	605
184	337	467-72	608-13
186-87	343	476	615
190	347-51	478	617

619	765	907	1047-48
622	767	909-18	1051-52
625-29	769-71	921	1054-56
631-33	774	923-26	1060
635-36	779	931-34	1062-63
638	781	936-37	1067-68
640	786-87	939	1076
642-46	795	942-48	1079
648-59	799-800	950-51	1081
661-63	802	954-55	1084-98
665-68	805	957	1100-1101
682-86	808	959	1104-8
688	810-16	961	1110-11
691-92	818-21	963-64	1113-15
694	827	966-70	1119-21
698	830	973-75	1124-28
700-702	832-41	979-87	1130-31
704	845-54	990-91	1133
709-10	856-57	993-96	1135-37
712-13	859	998	1140
716	861-62	1000-1001	1142-43
720-23	865-68	1006	1150-51
728-32	870-81	1009-20	1155
738-41	884	1029-31	1158-66
744	886-92	1034	1176-78
746	895-96	1036-38	1180-81
748-55	898-902	1040-41	1183-84
763	904-5	1045	

New Testament

1243	1280-82	1370	1395
1246	1292	1373	1397-1400
1248-53	1304	1376-77	1402
1274	1322-24	1379	1406-7
1276-78	1330	1386-87	1549

87

Appendix C

Location of "JST" Footnotes; Additional "JST" Excerpts

Under inspiration, Joseph Smith made thousands of changes in the King James text. Hundreds of excerpts from the Joseph Smith Translation are included in the new LDS edition of Bible, either on the pages where the corresponding KJV materials appear or in a special section of the Appendix (pp. 797-813). In order to help you place the JST excerpts in proper perspective in relationship to other major translations, a brief historical review of the Bible is included here.

The Bible has gone through many compilations and translations since the original books were prepared by the prophets or other writers. Even today different religious groups accept different books as comprising the text of the Old Testament. The Eastern Orthodox churches, for example, include some Old Testament books not accepted by most Protestants (the Apocrypha), and the Roman Catholics accept even more of the apocryphal writings than do the Eastern Orthodox groups.

Different translations of the Old Testament have affected profoundly the religious beliefs and customs of people accepting that particular translation. The Septuagint is an early Greek translation dating from the third and second centuries B.C. The Vulgate is a Latin translation prepared primarily under the direction of Jerome around A.D. 400 and used by the Roman Catholic Church for more than a thousand years.

Of the many English translations of the Bible, two have played a predominant role: for Catholics, the Reims-Douai Bible of 1582-1610 (commonly known as the Douai version); for Protestants, the King James Version of 1611, also known as the Authorized Version.

The Church of Jesus Christ of Latter-day Saints has officially sanctioned the use of the King James Version; reasons for this recommendation are found in *Why the King James Version* by J. Reuben Clark, Jr. (Deseret Book, 1979). Thus the text of the new edition of the Bible containing special aids for Latter-day Saints is the latest approved text of the King James Version.

Joseph Smith Translation

Another English biblical translation of particular interest to Latter-day Saints is the Joseph Smith Translation, also known by such designations as the Inspired Translation, Inspired Version, Inspired Revision, and the New Translation.

Early in this dispensation the Lord commanded his prophet, Joseph Smith, Jr., to prepare a new translation of the Old Testament and New Testament. (HC 1:238.) A major purpose of this new translation was to restore the "plain and precious truths" of the Bible that had been lost by "ignorant translators, careless transcribers, or evil and designing priests" who had caused many corruptions in the original text. (1 Ne. 13:26-40; *Teachings of the Prophet Joseph Smith*, p. 327.) Another purpose was to restore more nearly the original meaning of the scriptures as first written.

Several revelations in the Doctrine and Covenants and numerous entries in Joseph Smith's diary attest to the progress of the work through the 1830s and early 1840s. However, severe persecution, financial hardships, and other circumstances prevented the Prophet from finishing and publishing the translation in his lifetime.

In 1867 the Reorganized Church of Jesus Christ of Latter Day Saints (RLDS) published a version of the Bible containing most of the changes recommended by Joseph Smith under the title *Holy Scriptures.* In 1944 the RLDS published a "new corrected edition" under the title *Holy Scriptures: Inspired Edition.* An analysis of these editions and a wealth of background information pertaining to the Joseph Smith Translation are found in *Joseph Smith's Translation of the Bible—A History and Commentary* by Robert J. Matthews (Brigham Young University Press, 1975).

Although The Church of Jesus Christ of Latter-day Saints (Utah Mormons) has never officially sanctioned the use of the Joseph Smith Translation in its instructional and missionary programs, many leaders and members of the Church have quoted from it to explain difficult or ambiguous biblical passages.

Care should be taken in the use of the Joseph Smith Translation, however, as we are not always certain whether or not the Prophet had completed the translation of a particular verse. If a significant alteration is made in a verse, then we know the Prophet reviewed the verse and felt the change was necessary and essential. If no change is made in a verse, it may mean the verse is already complete and correct, or it may mean the Prophet had not completed analyzing that particular verse.

Additional care should be taken in making conclusions concerning the JST excerpts included in the new LDS edition of the Bible. For example, the first list below indicates the number of JST excerpts (*not* the number of verses) appearing in each of the sixty-six books of the new edition of the Bible. The fact that some books do not contain any JST excerpts may indicate either (1) Joseph Smith did not change any verses in that particular book, or (2) Joseph Smith made some changes in that book but they are not included in the new edition of the Bible.

Simply because there are no JST changes in the KJV text does not necessarily mean the text is whole, complete, or "translated correctly."

The following list indicates the number of JST excerpts found in the LDS edition of the Bible:

Old Testament

Gen., 28	Judg., 0	1 Chr., 1	Ps., 12
Ex., 29	Ruth, 0	2 Chr., 2	Prov., 1
Lev., 0	1 Sam., 6	Ezra, 0	Eccl., 0
Num., 1	2 Sam., 1	Neh., 2	Song., 0
Deut., 3	1 Kgs., 8	Esth., 0	Isa., 6
Josh., 0	2 Kgs., 0	Job, 2	Jer., 5

Lam., 0	Amos, 4	Hab., 0	
Ezek., 2	Obad., 0	Zeph., 0	
Dan., 1	Jonah, 2	Hag., 0	
Hosea, 1	Micah, 0	Zech., 2	
Joel, 2	Nahum, 0	Mal., 0	

New Testament

Matt., 81	2 Cor., 6	1 Tim., 5	2 Pet., 4
Mark, 38	Gal., 2	2 Tim., 2	1 Jn., 11
Luke, 65	Eph., 1	Titus, 2	2 Jn., 0
John, 38	Philip., 4	Philem., 0	3 Jn., 0
Acts., 13	Col., 3	Heb., 22	Jude, 2
Rom., 24	1 Thes., 4	James, 7	Rev., 20
1 Cor., 25	2 Thes., 4	1 Pet., 8	

Location of "JST" Excerpts

The following list identifies the pages of the Bible containing at least one JST footnote entry. This list should be helpful in marking those footnote entries.

Old Testament

10	113-14	575	912
12-14	130	607	925
19-26	133-34	662	934
30	219	679-80	937
33-34	270	719-21	978
60-61	277	725	983
74	402	728	1058-59
78	404-5	731-32	1109
81	408	746	1130
84	441	787	1134-35
86-88	484	805-6	1139
91-94	486	830	1143
99-100	489	895	1149
106	492	901	1173-74

New Testament

1187-99	1223-29	1245-48	1263
1201	1232	1251	1266-68
1204-11	1235	1253	1270-72
1216-18	1237	1255-59	1275
1220-21	1239-42	1261	1277-82

1284	1361-63	1450	1518
1288-89	1366	1452	1521
1291-92	1368	1454	1524-28
1294	1370	1456	1530-32
1296-1300	1373-74	1458	1534
1303-5	1378	1460	1538-40
1307-10	1381	1464-65	1544
1312	1390	1471	1547-49
1314	1397	1473-74	1552
1316-18	1401	1476	1554-56
1321-22	1406-7	1485	1558-59
1324	1416	1489	1561
1326-31	1419-21	1491-95	1563-66
1334-39	1423-24	1498	1568
1342-44	1426-28	1501	1570-72
1346-47	1433	1503-4	1575
1349	1435	1507-8	1577-78
1351	1437	1510	1585-86
1354	1439-43	1512	
1356	1445-47	1515-16	

Additional "JST" Excerpts

It was impossible to include in the new LDS edition of the King James text all the significant contributions of the Joseph Smith Translation, either as footnotes or in the special section of the Appendix. Hundreds of worthwhile contributions were included, but many others might have been included had space permitted.

Listed on the following pages are several additional quotations from the Joseph Smith Translation. The King James text is listed on the left side, identified by book, chapter, and verse (and by the page in the new edition of the Bible where the text appears). Corresponding quotations from the Joseph Smith Translation are listed on the right side of the page, identified by book, chapter, and verse. The italicized words might well be written into the King James text.

You might want to review each of these quotations to determine whether you feel the changes are significant enough to note in your copy of the King James text.

King James Version (KJV)

Joseph Smith Translation (JST)

Gen. 11:9 (p. 16)
Therefore is the name of it called
Babel; because the Lord did there
confound the language of all the
earth . . .

Gen. 11:6
. . . therefore, is the name of it called
Babel, because *the Lord was displeased
with their works,* and did there
confound the language of all the
earth . . .

Gen. 12:15 (p. 18)
. . . and commended her before
Pharaoh . . .

Gen. 12:11
. . . and *commanded* her to be brought
before Pharaoh . . .

Gen. 14:14 (p. 20)
And when Abram heard that his
brother was taken captive . . .

Gen. 14:13
And when Abram heard that Lot, *his
brother's* son, was taken captive . . .

Gen. 16:10 (p. 22)
And the angel of the Lord said unto
her, I will multiply thy seed
exceedingly . . .

Gen. 16:11
And the angel of the Lord said unto
her, *The Lord* will multiply thy seed
exceedingly . . .

Gen. 17:6 (p. 23)
. . . kings shall come out of thee.

Gen. 17:10
. . . kings shall come of thee, *and of thy
seed.*

Gen. 17:18 (p. 23)
. . . O that Ishmael might live before
thee!

Gen. 17:24
. . . Oh that Ishmael might live
uprightly before thee!

Gen. 18:20 (p. 25)
And the Lord said . . .

Gen. 18:19
And the *angel of the* Lord said . . .

Gen. 18:33 (p. 26)
And the Lord went his way, as soon
as he had left communing with
Abraham . . .

Gen. 18:41
And as soon as he had left
communing with the Lord, *Abraham
went his way.*

Gen. 19:11 (p. 26)
. . . they wearied themselves to find
the door.

Gen. 19:17
. . . they wearied themselves to find
the door, *and could not find it.*

Gen. 19:33 (p. 27)
And they made their father drink
wine . . .

Gen. 19:39
And they *did wickedly,* and made their
father drink wine . . .

93

King James Version (KJV)	Joseph Smith Translation (JST)
Gen. 21:6 (p. 29) And Sarah said, God hath made me to laugh, so that all that hear will laugh with me.	**Gen. 21:5** And Sarah said, God has made me to *rejoice;* and also all that know me will *rejoice* with me.
Gen. 21:21 (p. 30) . . . and his mother took him a wife out of the land of Egypt.	**Gen. 21:18-19** . . . and he dwelt in the wilderness of Paran, he and his mother. And *he took him a wife* out of the land of Egypt.
Gen. 22:1 (p. 31) . . . God did tempt Abraham . . .	**Gen. 22:1** . . . God did *try* Abraham . . .
Gen. 22:12 (p. 31) . . . thine only son from me.	**Gen. 22:15** . . . thine *only Isaac* from me.
Gen. 25:7 (p. 36) And these are the days of the years of Abraham's life . . .	**Gen. 25:7** And these are the *number* of the years of Abraham's life . . .
Gen. 29:21 (p. 44) . . . for my days are fulfilled.	**Gen. 29:21** . . . for my days *of serving thee* are fulfilled.
Gen. 48:10 (p. 74) Israel . . . could not see.	**Gen. 48:16** Israel . . . could not see *well.*
Exodus 12:33 (p. 97) . . . for they said, We be all dead men.	**Exodus 12:33** . . . for they said, *We have found our first-born all dead.*
Exodus 21:20 (p. 111) . . . he shall be surely punished.	**Exodus 21:20** . . . he shall surely be *put to death.*
Exodus 32:35 (p. 132) . . . they made the calf, which Aaron made.	**Exodus 32:35** . . . they *worshipped* the calf, which Aaron made.
Leviticus 21:11 (p. 178) Neither shall he go in to any dead body . . .	**Leviticus 21:11** Neither shall he go in *to touch* any dead body . . .

King James Version (KJV)	Joseph Smith Translation (JST)
Leviticus 22:9 (p. 179) . . . if they profane it: I the Lord do sanctify them.	Leviticus 22:9 . . . if they *profane not mine ordinances,* I the Lord will sanctify them.
Deuteronomy 2:30 (p. 256) . . . for the Lord thy God hardened his spirit . . .	Deuteronomy 2:30 . . . for *he hardened his spirit* . . .
Deuteronomy 34:6 (p. 308) And he buried him . . . but no man knoweth of his sepulchre unto this day.	Deuteronomy 34:6 For *the Lord took him unto his fathers,* . . . therefore no man knoweth of his sepulcher unto this day.
Joshua 11:20 (p. 324) For it was of the Lord to harden their hearts . . .	Joshua 11:20 For it was of the Lord to destroy them utterly, because *they hardened their hearts* . . .
Judges 2:18 (p. 346) . . . it repented the Lord because of their groanings . . .	Judges 2:18 . . . for the Lord *hearkened* because of their groanings . . .
1 Samuel 15:35 (p. 403) . . . the Lord repented that he had made Saul king over Israel.	1 Samuel 15:35 . . . the Lord *rent the kingdom from Saul* whom he had made king over Israel.
1 Samuel 19:9 (p. 409) And the evil spirit from the Lord . . .	1 Samuel 19:9 And the evil spirit which was *not* of the Lord . . .
1 Samuel 28:11 (p. 422) . . . And he said, Bring me up Samuel.	1 Samuel 28:11 And he said, Bring me up *the word of* Samuel.
2 Samuel 24:16 (p. 462) . . . the Lord repented . . .	2 Samuel 24:16 . . . *the people repented* . . .
1 Kings 3:1 (p. 468) And Solomon made affinity with Pharaoh king of Egypt . . .	1 Kings 3:1 And *the Lord was not pleased with Solomon,* for he made affinity with Pharaoh . . .

King James Version (KJV)

Joseph Smith Translation (JST)

1 Kings 3:12 (p. 469)
. . . there was none like thee before
thee . . .

1 Kings 3:12
. . . there was none *made king over
over Israel* like unto thee before
thee . . .

1 Kings 3:14 (p. 469)
And if thou wilt walk in my ways, to
keep my statutes and my
commandments, as thy father David
did walk, then I will lengthen thy
days.

1 Kings 3:14
And if thou wilt walk in my ways to
keep my statutes, and my
commandments, then I will lengthen
thy days, and *thou shalt not walk in
unrighteousness, as did thy father David.*

1 Kings 14:8 (p. 490)
And rent the kingdom away from
the house of David, and gave it thee:
and yet thou hast not been as my
servant David, who kept my
commandments . . .

1 Kings 14:8
And rent the kingdom away from the
house of David and gave it thee,
because he kept not my commandments.

1 Kings 15:5 (p. 492)
. . . save only in the matter of Uriah
the Hittite.

1 Kings 15:5
. . . save only in the matter of Uriah
the Hittite, *wherein the Lord cursed
him.*

2 Kings 19:35 (p. 538)
. . . and when they arose early in the
morning, behold, they were all dead
corpses.

2 Kings 19:35
. . . and when *they who were left* arose
early in the morning, behold, they
were all dead corpses.

2 Chronicles 18:20 (p. 607)
Then there came out a spirit . . .

2 Chronicles 18:20
Then there came out a *lying* spirit . . .

2 Chronicles 22:2 (p. 612)
Forty and two years old was Ahaziah
when he began to reign . . .

2 Chronicles 22:2
Two and twenty years old was Ahaziah
when he began to reign . . .

2 Chronicles 34:16 (p. 629-30)
And Shaphan . . . brought the king
word back again . . .

2 Chronicles 34:16
And Shaphan . . . brought *the word of
the king* back again . . .

Psalm 22:12 (p. 726)
Many bulls have compassed me:
strong bulls of Bashan . . .

Psalm 22:12
Many *armies* have compassed me;
strong *armies* of Bashan . . .

King James Version (KJV)

Joseph Smith Translation (JST)

Psalm 36:1 (p. 736)
The transgression of the wicked saith within my heart, that there is no fear of God before his eyes.

Psalm 36:1
The *wicked,* who live in transgression, *saith in their hearts,* There is no condemnation; for there is no fear of God before *their* eyes.

Psalm 82:2 (p. 768)
How long will ye judge unjustly . . .

Psalm 82:2
How long will ye *suffer them* to judge unjustly . . .

Psalm 102:18 (p. 780)
. . . the people which shall be created shall praise the Lord.

Psalm 102:18
. . . the people which shall be *gathered* shall praise the Lord.

Psalm 135:21 (p. 803)
Blessed be the Lord out of Zion, which dwelleth at Jerusalem.

Psalm 135:21
Blessed be the Lord *out of Zion;* Blessed be the Lord *out of Jerusalem.*

Isaiah 5:9 (p. 867)
. . . many houses shall be desolate, even great and fair, without inhabitant.

Isaiah 5:9
. . . many houses shall be desolate, and great and fair *cities* without inhabitant.

Isaiah 6:9 (p. 869)
. . . Hear ye indeed, but understand not; and see ye indeed, but perceive not.

Isaiah 6:9
. . . Hear ye indeed, but *they understood* not; and see ye indeed, but *they perceived not.*

Isaiah 13:15 (p. 878)
Every one that is found shall be thrust through;

Isaiah 13:15
Every one that is *proud* shall be thrust through;

Isaiah 14:19 (p. 880)
. . . and as the raiment of those that are slain . . .

Isaiah 14:19
. . . and the *remnant* of those that are slain . . .

Isaiah 29:10 (p. 895)
For the Lord . . . hath closed your eyes: the prophets and your rulers, the seers hath he covered.

Isaiah 29:10
For, behold *ye have closed your eyes, and ye have rejected the prophets,* and your rulers; and the seers hath he covered *because of your iniquities.*

King James Version (KJV)	Joseph Smith Translation (JST)
Isaiah 37:32 (pp. 905-6) . . . and they that escape out of mount Zion . . .	Isaiah 37:32 . . . and they that escape out of *Jerusalem shall come up* upon mount Zion . . .
Isaiah 51:20 (p. 924) Thy sons have fainted . . .	Isaiah 51:20 Thy sons have fainted *save these two* . . .
Jeremiah 2:24 (p. 944) . . . they shall find her.	Jeremiah 2:24 . . . they shall *not* find her.
Jeremiah 18:8 (p. 966) . . . I will repent of the evil . . .	Jeremiah 18:8 . . . I will *withhold* the evil . . .
Jeremiah 18:10 (p. 967) . . . I will repent of the good.	Jeremiah 18:10 . . . I will *withhold* the good . . .
Jeremiah 26:3 (p. 977) If so be they will hearken, and turn every man from his evil way, that I may repent me of the evil . . .	Jeremiah 26:3 If so be they will hearken, and turn every man from his evil way, and *repent*, I will turn away the evil . . .
Ezekiel 48:35 (p. 1099) . . . and the name of the city from that day shall be, The Lord is there.	Ezekiel 48:35 . . . and the name of the city from that day shall be called, *Holy; for* the Lord shall be there.
Matthew 5:6 (p. 1192) . . . for they shall be filled.	Matthew 5:8 . . . for they shall be filled *with the Holy Ghost.*
Matthew 5:13 (p. 1193) Ye are the salt of the earth . . .	Matthew 5:15 *I give unto you* to be the salt of the earth . . .
Matthew 5:14 (p. 1193) Ye are the light of the world . . .	Matthew 5:16 . . . *I give unto you* to be the light of the world . . .
Matthew 8:10 (p. 1199) When Jesus heard it, he marvelled, and said to them that followed . . .	Matthew 8:9 And when they that followed him, heard this, *they marvelled* . . .

King James Version (KJV)	Joseph Smith Translation (JST)

Matthew 10:16 (p. 1203)
. . . be ye therefore wise as serpents . . .

Matthew 10:14
. . . be ye therefore wise *servants* . . .

Matthew 12:15 (p. 1207)
But when Jesus knew it . . .

Matthew 12:13
But *Jesus knew when* they took counsel,

Matthew 13:5-6 (p. 1209)
. . . and forthwith they sprung up, because they had no deepness of earth:
And when the sun was up, they were scorched . . .

Matthew 13:5
. . . and forthwith they sprung up; and when the sun was up, *they were scorched, because they had no deepness of earth* . . .

Matthew 13:44 (p. 1211)
. . . the which when a man hath found, he hideth . . .

Matthew 13:46
. . . And when a man hath found a treasure which is hid, *he secureth it* . . .

Matthew 15:9 (p. 1213)
. . . teaching for doctrines the commandments of men.

Matthew 15:8
. . . teaching the doctrines *and* the commandments of men.

Matthew 18:19 (p. 1219)
. . . as touching any thing that they shall ask, it shall be done for them . . .

Matthew 18:19
. . . as touching any thing that they shall ask, *that they may not ask amiss*, it shall be done for them . . .

Matthew 25:12 (p. 1232)
. . . Verily I say unto you, I know you not.

Matthew 25:11
. . . Verily I say unto you, *Ye know me not.*

Matthew 25:29 (p. 1233)
For unto every one that hath shall be given, . . . but from him that hath not shall be taken away even that which he hath.

Matthew 25:29-30
For unto every one who hath *obtained other talents*, shall be given . . .
But from him that *hath not obtained other talents*, shall be taken away even that which he hath received.

Mark 1:5 (p. 1242)
. . . and were all baptized of him . . .

Mark 1:4
. . . and *many* were baptized of him . . .

King James Version (KJV)

Joseph Smith Translation (JST)

Mark 2:18 (p. 1244)
And the disciples of John and of the Pharisees used to fast: and they come and say unto him . . .

Mark 2:16
And *they came and said* unto him, The disciples of John and of the Pharisees used to fast . . .

Mark 7:4 (p. 1252)
. . . except they wash, they eat not.

Mark 7:4
. . . except they wash *their bodies*, they eat not.

Mark 8:12 (p. 1254)
. . . There shall no sign be given unto this generation.

Mark 8:12
. . . There shall no sign be given unto this generation, save *the sign of the prophet Jonah;* . . .

Mark 8:29 (p. 1255)
. . . And Peter answereth and saith unto him, Thou art the Christ.

Mark 8:31
And Peter answered and said unto him, Thou art the Christ, *the Son of the living God.*

Mark 9:50 (p. 1258)
. . . but if the salt have lost his saltness, wherewith will ye season it? . . .

Mark 9:50
For if the salt have lost his saltness, wherewith will ye season it? (*the sacrifice;*) . . .

Mark 15:36 (p. 1270)
And one ran and filled a spunge full of vinegar, and put it on a reed, and gave him to drink, saying, Let alone . . .

Mark 15:41
And one ran and filled a sponge full of vinegar, and put it on a reed and gave him to drink; *others spake,* saying, Let him alone . . .

Luke 1:28 (p. 1273)
And the angel came in unto her, and said, Hail, thou that art highly favoured, the Lord is with thee: blessed art thou among women.

Luke 1:28
And the angel came in unto her and said, Hail, *thou virgin,* who art highly favored of the Lord. The Lord is with thee, for *thou art chosen* and blessed among women.

Luke 8:18 (p. 1289)
. . . for whosoever hath, to him shall be given; and whosoever hath not . . .

Luke 8:18
. . . for whosoever *receiveth,* to him shall be given; and whosoever *receiveth not* . . .

King James Version (KJV)

Luke 10:32 (p. 1295)
. . . passed by on the other side.

Luke 13:17 (p. 1302)
. . . all the people rejoiced . . .

Luke 17:10 (p. 1308)
. . . we have done that which was our
duty to do.

Luke 21:17 (p. 1315)
And ye shall be hated of all men for
my name's sake.

Luke 22:31 (p. 1318)
. . . that he may sift you as wheat . . .

John 3:32 (p. 1329)
. . . and no man receiveth his
testimony.

John 5:31 (p. 1334)
If I bear witness of myself, my witness
is not true.

John 6:27 (p. 1336)
. . . which the Son of man shall give
unto you . . .

John 9:27 (p. 1344)
. . . ye did not hear: wherefore would
ye hear it again?

Romans 13:2 (p. 1433)
. . . shall receive to themselves
damnation.

Joseph Smith Translation (JST)

Luke 10:33
. . . passed by on the other side of the
way; for *they desired in their hearts that
it might not be known that they had seen
him.*

Luke 13:17
. . . all his *disciples* rejoiced . . .

Luke 17:10
. . . We have done that which was *no
more than our duty* to do.

Luke 21:16
And ye shall be hated *of all the world*
for my name's sake.

Luke 22:31
. . . that he may sift *the children of the
kingdom* as wheat.

John 3:32
. . . and but *few men* receive his
testimony.

John 5:32
Therefore if I bear witness of myself,
yet *my witness is true.*

John 6:27
. . . which the *Son of Man hath power*
to give unto you . . .

John 9:27
. . . ye did not *believe;* wherefore *would
you believe* if I should tell you again?

Romans 13:2
. . . shall receive to themselves
punishment.

King James Version (KJV)　　　　　*Joseph Smith Translation (JST)*

Romans 14:23 (p. 1435)
And he that doubteth is damned . . .

Romans 14:23
And he that doubteth is *condemned* . . .

1 Corinthians 1:12 (p. 1439)
. . . every one of you saith . . .

1 Corinthians 1:12
. . . *many* of you saith . . .

1 Corinthians 1:28 (p. 1440)
. . . to bring to nought things that are:

1 Corinthians 1:28
. . . to bring to naught things that are *mighty;*

1 Corinthians 12:31 (p. 1454)
But covet earnestly the best gifts: and yet shew I unto you a more excellent way.

1 Corinthians 12:31
. . . for I have shown unto you a more excellent way, therefore *covet* earnestly *the best gifts.*

2 Corinthians 5:18 (p. 1465)
And all things are of God . . .

2 Corinthians 5:18
And *receiveth* all the things of God . . .

Hebrews 11:24 (p. 1534)
. . . when he was come to years . . .

Hebrews 11:24
. . . when he was come to years *of discretion* . . .

Hebrews 12:12 (p. 1535)
. . . lift up the hands which hang down, and the feeble knees;

Hebrews 12:12
. . . lift up the hands which hang down, and *strengthen* the feeble knees;

Revelation 10:4 (p. 1575)
. . . Seal up those things . . .

Revelation 10:4
. . . Those things *are sealed up* . . .

In the following list the JST references contain significant changes from their KJV counterparts, but it was decided not to quote them in their entirety here. You might want to read the JST quotation, compare it with the corresponding KJV reference, and then decide whether or not you want to note the changes in your copy of the KJV text.

KJV	JST	KJV	JST
Gen. 10:9	Gen. 10:5	Gen. 14:13	Gen. 14:12
Gen. 10:21	Gen. 10:12	Gen. 15:1	Gen. 15:2
Gen. 13:13	Gen. 13:11	Gen. 16:13	Gen. 16:14-16
Gen. 14:10	Gen. 14:9	Gen. 17:1	Gen. 17:1

KJV	JST	KJV	JST
Gen. 18:3	Gen. 18:3	Zech. 6:5	Zech. 6:5
Gen. 18:10	Gen. 18:9	Matt. 10:14	Matt. 10:12
Gen. 18:16	Gen. 18:16	Matt. 12:49	Matt. 12:43-44
Gen. 19:1	Gen. 19:2	Matt. 15:5	Matt. 15:5
Gen. 19:16	Gen. 19:24	Matt. 23:39	Matt. 23:39-41
Gen. 19:24	Gen. 19:31	Matt. 25:26	Matt. 25:26
Gen. 19:31	Gen. 19:37	Matt. 26:45-46	Matt. 26:42-43
Gen. 20:16	Gen. 20:17	Matt. 27:24	Matt. 27:26
Gen. 21:7	Gen. 21:6	Matt. 27:52	Matt. 27:56
Gen. 22:6	Gen. 22:7	Matt. 27:64	Matt. 27:65
Gen. 24:5	Gen. 24:3	Mark 6:20	Mark 6:21
Gen. 24:28	Gen. 24:27	Mark 15:1	Mark 15:1-2
Gen. 38:8	Gen. 38:8	Luke 2:36	Luke 2:36
Ex. 5:4	Ex. 5:4	Luke 12:33	Luke 12:36
Ex. 6:8	Ex. 6:8	Luke 12:49	Luke 12:58
Ex. 9:17	Ex. 9:17	Luke 12:58	Luke 12:67
Ex. 20:23	Ex. 20:23	Luke 14:7	Luke 14:7
Ex. 33:1	Ex. 33:1	Luke 17:22	Luke 17:22
Num. 22:20	Num. 22:20	Luke 19:8	Luke 19:8
Deut. 16:22	Deut. 16:22	Luke 20:10	Luke 20:10
1 Kgs. 3:6	1 Kgs. 3:6	John 3:21	John 3:21-22
1 Kgs. 3:7	1 Kgs. 3:8	John 5:40	John 5:41
1 Kgs. 11:35	1 Kgs. 11:35	John 8:11	John 8:11
1 Kgs. 13:26	1 Kgs. 13:26	Rom. 1:9-10	Rom. 1:9-10
Ps. 10:10	Ps. 10:10	Rom. 1:20	Rom. 1:20
Ps. 10:16	Ps. 10:16	1 Cor. 11:19	1 Cor. 11:19
Ps. 12:1	Ps. 12:1	Gal. 1:10	Gal. 1:10
Ps. 12:5-8	Ps. 12:5-8	Gal. 1:24	Gal. 1:24
Ps. 32:3	Ps. 32:3	2 Tim. 2:8	2 Tim. 2:8
Ps. 36:5	Ps. 36:5	Heb. 11:23	Heb. 11:23
Ps. 39:9	Ps. 39:9	1 Pet. 2:7	1 Pet. 2:8
Ps. 90:13	Ps. 90:13	1 Pet. 4:4	1 Pet. 4:4
Ps. 112:8	Ps. 112:8	1 Jn. 5:13	1 Jn. 5:13
Isa. 2:5	Isa. 2:5	Rev. 19:5	Rev. 19:5
Isa. 2:21	Isa. 2:21		
Isa. 13:3	Isa. 13:3		
Isa. 13:22	Isa. 13:22		
Isa. 14:2	Isa. 14:2		
Isa. 37:36	Isa. 37:37		
Isa. 62:5	Isa. 62:5		
Amos 4:3	Amos 4:3		
Zech. 4:10	Zech. 4:10		

Reference Chart

The reference chart here is provided to help you keep a record for reference purposes of the various colors used to mark and/or color the various aspects of your Bible. In the headings at the top, write the colors you use. Then put a check in the column under that color, opposite the appropriate topic heading(s):

	Red											
GR Footnotes												
HEB Footnotes												
IE Footnotes												
JST Footnotes												
OR Footnotes												
Chapter Designations and Numbers												
Topical Guide Entries												
Bible Dictionary Entries												
JST Section Excerpts												
Gazetteer Entries												
Map Titles												

Matt.	Matthew	Genesis	Gen.
Mark	Mark	Exodus	Ex.
Luke	Luke	Leviticus	Lev.
John	John	Numbers	Num.
Acts	Acts	Deuteronomy	Deut.
Rom.	Romans	Joshua	Josh.
Cor.	1 & 2 Corinthians	Judges	Judg.
Gal.	Galatians	Ruth	Ruth
Eph.	Ephesians	1 Samuel	1 Sam.
Philip.	Philippians	2 Samuel	2 Sam.
Col.	Colossians	1 Kings	1 Kgs.
Thes.	1 & 2 Thessalonians	2 Kings	2 Kgs.
Tim.	1 & 2 Timothy	1 Chronicles	1 Chr.
Titus	Titus	2 Chronicles	2 Chr.
Philem.	Philemon	Ezra	Ezra
Heb.	Hebrews	Nehemiah	Neh.
James	James	Esther	Esth.
Pet.	1 & 2 Peter	Job	Job
Jn.	1, 2, & 3 John	Psalms	Ps.
Jude	Jude	Proverbs	Prov.
Rev.	Revelation	Ecclesiastes	Eccl.
		Song, Solomon	Song.
		Isaiah	Isa.

TG "A" Topical Guide

TG "H" Topical Guide

TG "R" Topical Guide

BD "A" Bible Dictionary

BD "Chronological Tables"

BD "Harmony of Gospels"

JST Joseph Smith Translation

Gaz.   Gazetteer

Genesis	Gen.
Exodus	Ex.
Leviticus	Lev.
Numbers	Num.
Deuteronomy	Deut.
Joshua	Josh.
Judges	Judg.
Ruth	Ruth
1 Samuel	1 Sam.
2 Samuel	2 Sam.
1 Kings	1 Kgs.
2 Kings	2 Kgs.
1 Chronicles	1 Chr.
2 Chronicles	2 Chr.
Ezra	Ezra
Nehemiah	Neh.
Esther	Esth.
Job	Job
Psalms	Ps.
Proverbs	Prov.
Ecclesiastes	Eccl.
Song, Solomon	Song.
Isaiah	Isa.
Jeremiah	Jer.
Lamentations	Lam.
Ezekiel	Ezek.
Daniel	Dan.
Hosea	Hosea
Joel	Joel
Amos	Amos
Obadiah	Obad.
Jonah	Jonah
Micah	Micah
Nahum	Nahum
Habakkuk	Hab.
Zephaniah	Zeph.
Haggai	Hag.
Zechariah	Zech.
Malachi	Mal.